Mrs. Rowe's *little book of* Southern Pies

Mrs. Rowe's

little
book of

Southern Pies

Mollie Cox Bryan &
Mrs. Rowe's Restaurant and Bakery

Photography by Jennifer Martiné

TEN SPEED PRESS
Berkeley

Library of Congress Cataloging-in-Publication Data

Bryan, Mollie Cox, 1963-
    Mrs. Rowe's little book of Southern pies / by Mollie Cox
Bryan and Mrs. Rowe's Restaurant and Bakery.
        p. cm.
    Includes index.
    Summary: "A sweet collection of sixty recipes for pie from
the famous family-owned Shenandoah Valley institution, Mrs.
Rowe's Restaurant and Bakery"—Provided by publisher.
    1. Pies. 2. Cookery, American—Southern style. 3. Mrs.
Rowe's Restaurant and Bakery. I. Mrs. Rowe's Restaurant and
Bakery. II. Title.
    TX773.B8835 2009
    641.5975—dc22
                                            2008037779

ISBN 978-1-58008-980-7

Printed in China

Design by Katy Brown
Food styling by Kim Konecny
Prop styling by Christine Wolheim

11 10 9 8 7 6 5

First Edition

For my daughters, Emma Aine and Tess Mathilde,
my own sweet little pie makers and eaters.

Also for my mom, Sandy, a master pumpkin pie baker.

Contents

Acknowledgments

First a great big thanks goes to my husband, Eric—always there for me and for pie, as are my daughters, Emma and Tess. At this point, they can all tell you everything you need to know about Mrs. Rowe, pie, or the restaurant.

Special thanks goes to Kate Antea, our pie tester, whose talent, patience, and observations added a great deal of depth to this book. Thanks to Chef William Poole of Wen Chocolates for letting us borrow Kate from her work from time to time to test pie. I understand that Kate's sister Bevin and her colleagues "endured" countless hours of pie tasting—so a big thanks goes to them.

I'd also like to send out a big thanks to my agent, Angela Miller, for her patience, unique observations, and her encouragement on all fronts.

Thanks to Michael DiGrassie, Aaron DiGrassie, and the whole Rowe-DiGrassie clan. Thanks to Angie Bedlinsky, Cynthia Craig, and Susan Simmons, Mrs. Rowe's bakers, for answering my pie questions—over and over again. Thanks to Mrs. Brown for sharing recipes.

Also, a few of my writer friends read the manuscript and offered suggestions— Alice Leonhardt and Elizabeth Massie. I am honored to know them and count them as my friends. Christy Majors, another good friend who I am honored to know, also read the manuscript, and I thank her for finding time in her hectic schedule.

Thanks to Esther Shank, Stephanie Witmer, Kendra Bailey Morris, John T. Edge, and Lorna Reeves, food writers and editors who were all generous with their time and thoughts. Thanks to Karen Becker and David Puckett of the Frontier Culture Museum in Staunton, Virginia, for filling me in on the history of pie safes.

I'd also like to acknowledge Aaron Wehner, editorial director at Ten Speed Press. This little book was his vision, and I want to thank him for his faith in me—and in the restaurant. I am thrilled, once again, to be a part of the Ten Speed team. A heartfelt thanks to the countless supporters who bought, reviewed, or otherwise supported *Mrs. Rowe's Restaurant Cookbook: A Lifetime of Recipes from the Shenandoah Valley*, which certainly helped pave the way for this new book. This most assuredly includes Kristin Casemore, publicist extraordinaire—thanks so much for your hard work.

I have been twice blessed by Ten Speed editors. Lisa Westmoreland's questions and directions provided a much needed focus for this book. I thank her for her generous, professional, and kind nature while editing this book. Thank you to copy editor Jasmine Star and designer Katy Brown, photographer Jennifer Martiné, food stylist Kim Konecny, and prop stylist Christine Wolheim.

Thank you to Antonia Allegra, who told me about the movie *Waitress*, which I found incredibly inspiring. What a great movie about pie and the power of mother-daughter love. After all, crafting a pie is basically about love—Mrs. Rowe knew that. If she were here today, I'd like to think she'd wink and smile about this book. So a very special thanks to the lady who started it all is in order. As long as we make her recipes, Mrs. Rowe lives in our hearts, minds, and satisfied bellies.

—Mollie

Introduction

Virginia is for lovers . . . of pie.

—PASCALE LE DRAOULEC, *AMERICAN PIE: SLICES OF LIFE*
(AND PIE) FROM AMERICA'S BACK ROADS

When I bite into a slice of coconut cream pie at Mrs. Rowe's Restaurant and Bakery, in Staunton, Virginia, I know where I am. One taste tells me with extraordinary smooth and rich flavors that take me home—or what I'd like home to be—a place of warmth and comfort where mothers and grandmothers fawn over me with delicious temptations from the oven. "One more slice, honey. Everything will be all right." Another bite and I absolutely believe it. That is the magic and glory of pie.

Pie takes you home even when you're sitting at a table in a restaurant that seats 250 and serves half a million meals a year. Even the waitresses buzzing around, the countless murmuring conversations, and the clanking of dishes and silverware don't detract from the ultimate pie experience. No food conjures images of home and hearth the way that pie does.

Pie is center stage when you walk into Mrs. Rowe's Staunton eatery, one of the most successful family-owned restaurants in the state of Virginia, a family business since 1947. Glass cases brim with puffy meringues, some dotted generously with chocolate chips, some just nicely browned, enticing eaters to wonder what delicious secrets lie beneath the sugary mounds. Often passing glances turn into stares as the hostess attempts to get people seated.

"What kind of pie is that?" one man wants to know. "Lemon meringue? Coconut Cream? Chocolate? Butterscotch?"

Answer: all of the above.

Pie. Some are born to make it; it's in the flick of their wrist, the intuitive touch in the tips of their fingers, and exacting instincts about how it should taste, look, smell, and even feel in the mouth.

Mildred Rowe was one of those people, blessed with sensitive, practiced hands and an extraordinary palate. She gladly filled the role of "Pie Lady," a nickname her customers gave her. Her green eyes sparkled, her hands went to her hips, and a smile spread across her face. "If you want some of that blackberry pie, you'd better order it now." Knowing that the specialty, seasonal pies would go fast, Mildred advised her customers to order dessert before anything else—just one of her personal touches that made customers feel special. Of course, that it was good for business did not escape her.

Mildred's extraordinary pies became legendary. Even as she earned the title of the undisputed "Queen of Pie" in the Shenandoah Valley, and maybe the state, she never took her role for granted. She was always seeking better recipes, better ingredients, and better financial success, balancing good food, reasonable prices, and staff management with the need to earn a living.

Now that Mildred is gone, her family and staff carry on. They strive for balance and efficiency in a constantly fluctuating business environment. Now the balancing act includes holding true to Mildred's vision while meeting the growing demands of over half a million increasingly younger customers each year.

Pie is one of the mainstays that has allowed the business to expand. Mildred once served slices of coconut cream, strawberry rhubarb, or chocolate pie to restaurant customers exclusively. Then, seeing a business opportunity, she began to sell whole pies to other local restaurants. At least four restaurants now buy whole pies from Mrs. Rowe's. Whole pies are also sold to locals on a regular basis, especially around the winter holidays.

The homemade pies Mildred made famous remain the most popular dessert at her restaurant. Throughout much of the country, pie is passé, having given way to fancy desserts like mousse, crème brûlée, and the inevitable biscotti lining coffee shop counters. But at Mrs. Rowe's, in the heart of Virginia's Shenandoah Valley, pie has never gone out of fashion.

Maybe it's the way the valley is wedged between the Alleghenies and the Blue Ridge, but change takes its time here, where folks still make a date for pie and a plain cup of coffee. With its paneled walls, homey green-checked placemats and menus, Windsor chairs, and lacy curtains, it's the kind of establishment that provides the perfect backdrop for catching up with family and friends. And if customers are lucky, Tootie McLear, an employee of thirty-five years, will be perched behind the cash register to fill them in on the weather and the latest local news—or she'll just smile and look pretty.

Mike DiGrassie, Mrs. Rowe's son and heir, and the general manager and owner of Mrs. Rowe's Restaurant and Bakery, moves around behind the counter, watching over the food as it comes out of the kitchen much the same way his mother did (except she sat on a stool). One minute he's at the register helping out, the next he's flying into the kitchen, and the next he's packing up a bag of Mrs. Rowe's delicious cookies to go.

Mrs. Rowe's restaurant business has more than doubled in the years since her death. Mike, his wife Mary Lou, and their son Aaron created M & M Management, which is the umbrella organization for all of their interests. Not only does Mike manage two restaurants—the newer one is Mrs. Rowe's Country Buffet in Mount Crawford—he has also expanded the business to include three cafeterias at local businesses and a catering company. Mary Lou, who manages the burgeoning catering arm, says its most requested desserts are the mini-pies. Mike, Mary Lou, and Aaron are passionate about the family business and about keeping up the quality of the food, especially the pie—mini or not.

Pie is just as popular at Mrs. Rowe's Country Buffet, located in the middle of Virginia's Mennonite community, as it is at Mrs. Rowe's Restaurant and Bakery. The pies stand on their own island, across from the long buffet tables of sweet sauerkraut, mashed potatoes, lima beans, fried chicken, and other American fare. The pies offer a cascade of color, from the deep brown of chocolate to the light tan of peanut butter, and from the golden hues of custards and lemon pies to the red, purple, and yellow shades of fruit-filled pies with juices spilling out the side. Already sliced, these pies sinfully lure innocent passersby. "We have customers

Pie Tips from Mrs. Rowe's Bakers and Our Recipe Tester, Kate

- For pies with a top crust, use an egg wash to create a nice golden brown hue.

- If you're going to fill a pie shell with a cooked filling, prick the crust with a fork to keep it from bulging up in the middle. This will help keep the shell level in the bottom and on the sides.

- Fruit pies have a tendency to run over, so always place the pie on a rimmed baking sheet for baking. It's a good idea to do this for all pies—just in case.

- Chill all rolled dough; the resting time lets the gluten relax. Cold dough is less likely to shrink as it bakes. The dough will hold its shape, then the fat melts and produces steam pockets, which make it flaky. So, cold dough + hot oven = flaky, nonshrinking crust.

- Let frozen pies stand at room temperature for five minutes before cutting.

- Custard fillings continue to cook when the pie is taken out of the oven, so don't overdo it.

- Pies are usually best served at room temperature (except for frozen and cold pies, of course). You can refrigerate them to preserve them longer, but remove them from the refrigerator about an hour before mealtime to create a more fresh-baked quality.

- To keep the crust from shrinking or bubbling during prebaking or parbaking, place a sheet of parchment on the pie crust and weight it down with dry beans or pie weights.

- The amount of liquid needed in a pie crust can depend on the weather. On a dry day you need more, on a wet day you need less. So try putting in one-half to two-thirds of the total amount of liquid, then see where the dough is and add more liquid as needed in tiny increments.

The Mrs. Rowe's restaurants sell 35,000 pies a year.

The restaurants make 3,000 gallons of meringue and use:

- 36,500 pounds of sugar
- 25,000 pounds of flour
- 20,000 pounds of butter

who eat three or four slices of pie every time they come in," says Susan Simmons, once the kitchen manager at the buffet, who now works for the catering branch. "It's incredible, but true."

Mrs. Rowe's Country Buffet is located off Interstate 81, twenty miles north of the Staunton restaurant. Aaron DiGrassie, Mike's son and Mildred's grandson, is the general manager. A chef by training, he stays in the kitchen, either overseeing the cooking and baking or doing it himself. His wife, Nicole, a new mother of the DiGrassies' only grandchild, is the business manager.

At Mrs. Rowe's Country Buffet, travelers get a real slice of Shenandoah Valley life alongside their slice of pie. While the restaurant is popular with locals who live contemporary lives, it is also a favorite with some Old Order Mennonites. The ladies wear white prayer caps and modest, simple dresses. The men also wear plain outfits. Some are family farmers. Some drive automobiles, while others depend on a horse and buggy. They all enjoy eating pie at Mrs. Rowe's Country Buffet. They feel welcome in the down-home country atmosphere, where cookie jars line the walls and silk flowers adorn every table.

This book includes several Mennonite pies, most notably the shoofly pie, which reflects the Pennsylvania German influence in Virginia. The Mennonites are keepers of Pennsylvania German foodways because of their general shunning of modern conveniences like electricity and therefore refrigerators. Today, Old Order Mennonites, the strictest group within the religion, still have no electricity. As a result, the recipes have changed little over the years since the mid-1700s, when the Shenandoah Valley's Mennonite population, masters of this pie, came down from Pennsylvania to Virginia, where land was cheaper and more plentiful. Shoofly pie became a traditional treat in this part of the South, along with a few other pies, including raisin and sour cream and raisin.

This book also includes a regional recipe that might surprise some readers: the Old-Fashioned Monterey Maple Syrup Pie. Although most people think of states like Vermont when they think of maple syrup, Virginia has its own sweet stock of it, especially in the "Little Switzerland" of Monterey, in Highland County. Southerners have been tapping maple trees for generations—and often getting a head start on their Northern neighbors. They can start tapping in January or February, whereas Northern tappers must wait until March.

Of course, this book also contains many of the signature pies of Mrs. Rowe's Restaurant and Bakery, including a few classics that first appeared in *Mrs. Rowe's Restaurant Cookbook: A Lifetime of Recipes from the Shenandoah Valley*. And finally, this book features some "attic classics"—recipes discovered in hand-scribbled notebooks and dusty recipe boxes, published for the first time in these pages. Bertha, Mildred's sister, who chronicled the family recipes, had a notebook that was especially fruitful. Willard Rowe, Mildred's second husband, also kept a small black notebook full of recipes and restaurant management notes, which yielded recipes including his namesake Willard's Chocolate Pie.

Most Popular Pies at Mrs. Rowe's Restaurant and Bakery

1. Original Coconut Cream Pie
2. Chocolate Meringue Pie

Most Popular Pies at Mrs. Rowe's Country Buffet

1. Peanut Butter Pie
2. French Apple Pie

Defining a vast and diverse region by its pie was a daunting task. I am merely a writer intrigued with Southern food and its stories. I searched and searched for a definition of "Southern" pie that spoke to me and rang true in my heart. Southern cook, baker, and cookbook author extraordinaire, Damon Lee Fowler, penned a definition of Southern baking in *New Southern Baking: Classic Flavors for Today's Cook*. I think it's a perfect description of "Southern" pie: "Its strength and beauty, like so much of the South's rich jazz, blues, country, and gospel music traditions, lies in its blending."

Hallelujah, and please pass me another slice.

Mrs. Rowe's Baking Tips

- Always read the recipe through first, checking to see if you have all of the ingredients. Assemble the ingredients and utensils.

- Margarine may be substituted for butter, but it's no substitute for flavor.

- Eggs give more volume when used at room temperature. Large eggs weigh about 2 ounces. If small eggs are used when large eggs are called for, the batter won't be the right consistency. Always use large eggs for the recipes in this book. When the recipe calls for separating eggs, the whites should be beaten until very stiff before folding them into the batter; then fold them in gently, just until there are no remaining patches of white.

- To measure dry ingredients, heap the ingredient in the cup or spoon, then level with the back of a knife. When measuring flour, don't shake the cup, as this can pack in the flour and add as much as an extra tablespoon or two of flour.

- Preheat the oven and always place pans in the center of the oven, on the center rack.

BASIC EQUIPMENT AND TECHNIQUES

For the home baker, much of this equipment is expendable. If you bake plenty of pies, investing in some tools will simply make your baking more efficient. Alongside the information about the tools, I have also given a more thrifty method. I have also included some basic pie techniques, in case pie baking is a new undertaking for you.

Pastry blender: This inexpensive kitchen tool, also sometimes called a pastry cutter, will cut down your time for making pie crust. You can also use it for dishes like mashed potatoes and guacamole. It has several U-shaped wires that connect to a straight handle. One of the most important benefits of a pastry blender is that it

stays cool—unlike your hands. (The more the shortening melts, the less flaky the crust will be.) After you dice your butter and shortening into smaller bits with a knife, toss them into the dry ingredients bowl and start cutting the tiny pieces with your blender. For standard pie crust, your work with the pastry blender is finished when the butter-flour mix resembles coarse cornmeal. However, Mrs. Rowe never used a pastry blender, which proves that you can make a superb crust using just forks and your hands.

Double boiler: Many of Mrs. Rowe's recipes call for a double boiler, which allows eggs and other heat-sensitive sauce ingredients to heat slowly and evenly. Chocolate must almost always be melted in a double boiler because direct heat will cause the temperature to rise too quickly, ruining the consistency. The restaurant, of course, uses huge double boilers, but they come in many sizes. They look like one pan sitting inside of another—and that's basically what they are. Chances are, you can just as easily devise your own using two pans—if one fits nicely into the other. Or you could use a large pan and a sturdy glass or stainless steel bowl that fits into it.

Parbaking: A good option for pie filling that doesn't bake long or is very wet, like the Old-Fashioned Monterey Maple Syrup Pie (page 112), or the Brown Sugar Pie (page 102), is parbaking the crust. This means partially baking and then cooling the crust before filling it and baking it again. It can take 10 to 20 minutes; the crust is ready when it starts to get a golden hue. Every oven is different so some vigilance is required. This helps prevent a soggy bottom crust.

Pie shields: Any kind of baked pie might need pie shields; the only way to know is to keep an eye on the pie. If the edges are browning too quickly, use shields. The most efficient pie shield is the kind that comes in four pieces so it can be adjusted to any size pie. The pieces stack for storage and take up almost no space. It's also easy to place them on a hot pie. The ones that come in rings are not one-size-fits-all, no matter what the package says, so you need one for each pie plate size. Foil is effective, cheap, fast, and an item the home baker should always have on hand. Just take a long piece of foil, fold it over until it's about three inches wide, and wrap it around the edges of the pie (which will probably be in the oven and hot at this point, so be careful). Do not cover the crust before you start baking because it will interfere with the crust setting up properly. If the crust is prebaked, it is okay to put the pie shield on before baking the filling.

Pie weights: Pie weights are sets of small weights that are designed to be placed into a pie crust for prebaking or parbaking. In addition to pie weights, which are available at many kitchen supply stores, home bakers can also use things like beans or rice to weight their pie crusts. There are several different kinds of pie weights.

One of the simplest is just a chain or set of beads strung together. The advantage of strung pie weights is that they are easy to handle and wash, and they will not be lost in a kitchen drawer somewhere. Home bakers can also use ceramic balls, polished river stones, or metal balls, in which case they typically come with a container for storage so that they will not be lost. To use pie weights, prepare the crust as directed, press it into the pie plate, pierce it several times for ventilation, and then arrange the pie weights evenly inside. Some cooks like to lay the pie weights on a coffee filter or piece of parchment paper so that they do not make impressions in the crust. After the pie is prebaked or parbaked, the pie weights are removed and the filling is poured or spooned in.

Scalding: Scalding milk used to mainly be done for safety reasons. But with modern pasteurization, it's not really necessary. Scalding enhances and infuses certain flavors, like vanilla and pumpkin, which is why it's called for in the Spicy Pumpkin Pie recipe (page 48). Scalding means bringing the milk to a simmer, almost a boil. The milk almost smells burned. Pay close attention—the milk will burn and boil over very quickly.

Sealing: All double-crusted pies are sealed by moistening the rim of the bottom crust with water or egg wash, laying the other crust on top, pressing the two layers together with your thumbs, and trimming the extra edges off. If a pie is simply sealed, the top may pop off. So pies should be crimped or fluted as well. The easiest way to crimp is to use the tines of a fork to press the rims of the crust down. The easiest way to flute is to create an even, raised dough edge around the rim, forming the raised dough into little Vs around the rim.

Vents: Double-crusted pies should have slits, cuts, or holes in the top. These vents allow steam to escape, and let you test for doneness by poking the filling without damaging the crust. You can get creative with your vents, making little designs in them or cutting out little shapes. Or simply make a center hole. As long as the steam can get out, not much else matters. It's a matter of personal preference—there's no "right" way to do it.

PANTRY NOTES

Brown sugar: Use light brown sugar, packed down, unless otherwise specified.

Butter: Always use unsalted, unless the recipe says otherwise.

Eggs: Always use large eggs when baking, unless the recipe says otherwise.

Flour: Use all-purpose flour for all of the recipes in this book.

Milk: Use whole milk, unless the recipe says otherwise.

White sugar: Use granulated.

Thanks for the Pie!

It's a country tradition to send sweets to your neighbors in times of need or celebration. The restaurants carry on this tradition that Mrs. Rowe felt was so important. Her personal papers are full of thank-you notes from folks who received some of her goodies.

"Thanks so much for the chocolate pie. We really enjoyed it."

—Mary Frances

"What a delicious pie! A most delightful surprise! We ate a slice and hid the rest in case someone in our family might come in and gobble it up."

—Dorothy and John

"Willie and I sure did enjoy the pie you gave us . . . I even had vanilla ice cream in the freezer. I guess it was waiting on something special to go with it."

—Willie and Ruth

Posted in the Kitchen at Mrs. Rowe's Country Buffet:

NOTICE TO ALL PIE STAFF·

Please do not cut more than one type of pie at a time. (Ex. Only one apple at a time, and so on.)

When using pies out of the larger refrigerator, take pies from the top shelf first and work your way down.

Older fruit pies are on the racks by the baking station. These are to be used first.

CHAPTER 1

Crusts and Toppings

Mrs. Rowe's is the house that pies built. No one has
ever managed to put more inches of meringue on
a pie—ever: *homemade* meringue, no less.

—LARRY BLY, *ROANOKE TIMES*

SIX EQUAL SLICES

Along with luscious pie toppings, this section offers basic crust recipes and creative
options for home bakers who are either strapped for time or crust-shy for other reasons. Experiment with the easy cookie crusts, which are not only quick and delicious, but also completely child-friendly. Both the Chocolate Cookie Crust (page
21) and the Gingersnap Crust (page 22) complement many fillings. Try the Chocolate Cookie Crust with the Smoothest Ever Peanut Butter Pie (page 82) or the

Gingersnap Crust with Willard's Chocolate Pie (page 80). Imagine the possibilities and don't be afraid to mix and match unexpected crusts and toppings—you might just come up with a winner.

A tiny, ball of energy of a woman, Mildred Rowe made everything seem easy with her quick wit and magic hands. But she was well practiced, having grown up on a farm in the Allegheny Highlands where everything was made from scratch or plucked straight from the earth. Not everybody grew up baking pies like Mrs. Rowe, but with practice and patience, it's a skill easily learned.

Because pie has become an increasingly important niche at Mrs. Rowe's Restaurant and Bakery and Mrs. Rowe's Country Buffet, the ritual of making and even cutting the pie is taken seriously at both restaurants. Indeed, it's a rite of privilege and honor to be trained to cut the pie. "You have to work here awhile before we even consider training you on cutting pie," says Mike DiGrassie, smiling, about the Staunton Mrs. Rowe's. "Cutting six equal slices is not as easy as it seems." He also points out that slicing through a mound of meringue neatly is a bit tricky for the novice. The crust is also an important focus according to Mike, who notes, "If the crust doesn't get cut through just right, the pie will tear and we won't be able to serve it." He recommends waiting until the pie has fully cooled, then cutting it with a blunt-tip serrated knife dipped in hot water.

At Mrs. Rowe's Country Buffet, the focus is more on variety and less on huge portions. Slices of fruit pies are cut smaller, allowing two more slices out of each pie. Ten-inch cream pies allow ten slices. "The nature of a buffet is that people keep going back for more," explains Aaron DiGrassie. "With the pie, they want to try each kind, so we keep the slices a little smaller."

The toppings and sauces at both restaurants provide an extra hint of sweetness or smoothness, or a blast of flavor, on top of a slice of pie that's already delicious.

BASIC CRUST TIPS

Placing beans on the crust before inserting into the oven is a good way to keep the crust from popping up unevenly.

Handle the dough as little as possible.

Roll the pie crust dough as flat and smooth as possible.

Smooth the crust gently into the pie plate.

You can use pastry scissors, other clean scissors, or your fingers to trim the crust.

Gather the dough into a border and squeeze into shape.

CRUSTS

Plain Pie Pastry

MAKES TWO 9- OR 10-INCH CRUSTS

Mildred's light touch took years to master. Too much flour will make the dough tough. Use just enough to keep it from sticking to the rolling pin. Make the dough ahead of time and place it in the refrigerator wrapped tightly in plastic wrap. If you don't have a pastry blender, you can use a fork here, as well as your fingers—if you start with cold hands and work fast. The more the shortening melts, the less flaky the crust will be.

Sift the flour and salt into a bowl. Cut in the shortening with a pastry blender until it is the size of small peas. Sprinkle 1 tablespoon of the milk over part of the flour mixture. Gently toss with a fork and push to the side of the bowl. Sprinkle another tablespoon over another dry part, toss with a fork and push to the side of the bowl. Repeat with the remaining milk until all of the flour mixture is moistened.

Press the dough together to form 2 equal balls, then flatten into disks. Roll out the crusts right away, or wrap the dough tightly, smoothing out any little wrinkles or air pockets, and refrigerate for up to 2 weeks. On a lightly floured surface, roll out each ball to a thickness of ⅛ inch. Use a light touch and handle the dough as little as possible.

2 cups all-purpose flour

1 teaspoon salt

⅔ cup vegetable shortening

5 to 7 tablespoons cold whole milk

(continued)

To prebake an empty crust, preheat the oven to 400°F. Press 1 rolled-out crust into a 9- or 10-inch pie plate. Line with parchment paper and weigh the crust down with dry beans or pie weights to keep the crust from bubbling or shrinking. Bake for 10 minutes, until firm and lightly browned. Take the crust out of the oven and carefully remove the pie weights. Place the crust back into the oven. To parbake the crust, remove it from the oven after about 10 to 20 minutes, when you first see a golden hue to the crust. To fully bake the crust, continue baking until golden brown, about 10 to 15 minutes more.

A notice posted in the kitchen at Mrs. Rowe's Country Buffet:

HOW PIES ARE CUT:

Cut all fruit pies and Boston cream pies into eight slices. This includes peach, apple, all sugar-free pies, strawberry rhubarb, cherry, red raspberry, blueberry, French apple, Boston cream. And egg custard.

Cut all meringue pies and pecan pies into ten slices. This includes lemon, coconut, chocolate, peanut butter, and butterscotch.

Vinegar Pie Crust

MAKES TWO 9-INCH CRUSTS

The vinegar in this crust is a flavorless stabilizer, making the dough more forgiving and patchable. In addition to being easy to work with, it also tastes great—even butter-loving pastry fans enjoy the flavor.

Sift the flour and salt into a bowl. Cut in the shortening with a pastry blender until it is the size of small peas. Add the vinegar, egg, and just enough ice water to moisten the dry ingredients.

Form the dough into 2 equal balls, then flatten into disks. Roll out the crusts right away, or wrap the dough tightly and refrigerate for up to 2 weeks. On a lightly floured surface, roll out each ball to a thickness of ⅛ inch.

To prebake an empty crust, preheat the oven to 400°F. Press 1 rolled-out crust into a 9- or 10-inch pie plate. Line with parchment paper and weight the crust down with dry beans or pie weights to keep the crust from bubbling or shrinking. Bake for 10 minutes, until firm and lightly browned. Take the crust out of the oven and carefully remove the pie weights. Place the crust back into the oven. To parbake the crust, remove it from the oven after 10 to 20 minutes, when you first see a golden hue to the crust. To fully bake the crust, continue baking until golden brown, about 10 to 15 minutes more.

2 cups all-purpose flour

½ teaspoon salt

1 cup plus 1 tablespoon vegetable shortening

1½ teaspoons distilled white vinegar

1 egg, lightly beaten

4 to 6 tablespoons ice water

Cream Cheese Crust

MAKES ONE 9-INCH CRUST

This crust, which has a nice tangy flavor, can be used in any recipe that calls for Plain Pie Pastry (page 17) or Vinegar Pie Crust (page 19). It's a good idea to chill the crust for at least 15 minutes before baking; this will help the crust stick together better.

½ cup cream cheese, at room temperature

½ cup unsalted butter, at room temperature

1½ cups all-purpose flour

Mix the cream cheese and butter together with an electric mixer on low speed until thoroughly combined. Add the flour a little at a time and continue mixing until thoroughly combined. The dough will be very crumbly. Press the dough together and smooth it over with your hands.

Shape the dough into a round disk and roll it out between 2 sheets of waxed paper to a thickness of ⅛ inch. Mend any cracks as you go along. If you have time, freeze the crust for 10 to 15 minutes before placing it in a pie plate for parbaking. If you don't have time to freeze, it's okay, but you still need to parbake this crust.

Preheat the oven to 350°F. Lift off the top sheet of waxed paper and use the bottom sheet to flip the dough into the pie plate. Remove the second sheet of waxed paper and prick the center of the crust with a fork. To parbake the crust, remove it from the oven after 10 to 20 minutes, when you first see a golden hue to the crust. To fully bake the crust, leave in the oven for another 10 minutes or until the crust is golden brown.

Chocolate Cookie Crust

MAKES ONE THICK 9-INCH CRUST OR ONE THIN 10-INCH CRUST

A simple pie crust with countless creative possibilities, the Chocolate Cookie Crust has been paired with the Frozen Strawberry Margarita Pie (page 90) and Grasshopper Pie (page 94) in this book, but also consider using it with any of the lemon or peanut butter pies, or even the Spicy Pumpkin Pie (page 48). You can crush the crumbs using a food processor, rolling pin, or kitchen mallet. This crust should be baked before filling.

Preheat the oven to 375°F.

Combine the crumbs and butter and mix well. Firmly and evenly press the mixture into a 9- or 10-inch pie plate.

Bake for 8 to 10 minutes, until the crust darkens to a deeper (almost black) brown, then cool on a wire rack for at least 30 minutes before filling. This crust can be made a day ahead and stored in the refrigerator.

2 cups crushed plain chocolate cookies
(without icing or filling)
6 tablespoons unsalted butter, melted

> When I have leftover cookies,
> I often use them in my crust.
>
> —SUSAN SIMMONS, BAKER AT
> MRS. ROWE'S CATERING

Gingersnap Crust

MAKES ONE 9-INCH CRUST

This versatile crust, which is extremely easy to make, adds zip to any pie, and its enticing flavor offers many intriguing possibilities. In this book it's paired with the Never Fail Lemon Pie (page 73), but you can also try it with pies like Cinnamon Sugar (page 84), Willard's Chocolate (page 80), German Chocolate (page 79), Peanut Butter Custard (page 83), Peanut (page 92), or Layered Ice Cream (page 96). You can crush the crumbs using a food processor, rolling pin, or kitchen mallet. This crust should be baked before being filled.

½ cup plus 2 tablespoons fine gingersnap crumbs

¾ cup plus 2 tablespoons fine graham cracker crumbs

2 tablespoons sugar

¼ cup unsalted butter, melted

Preheat the oven to 325°F.

Put the crumbs in a small bowl and stir in the sugar. Pour the melted butter over the crumbs and mix thoroughly. Press the mixture evenly into a 9-inch pie plate.

Bake for 5 to 6 minutes, until slightly darker, then cool on a wire rack for at least 30 minutes before filling. This crust can be made a day ahead and stored in the refrigerator.

"Pie crust promises . . . easily made and easily broken."

——MARY POPPINS

Graham Cracker Crust

MAKES ONE 9-INCH CRUST

You can crush the crumbs using a food processor, rolling pin, or kitchen mallet, whichever you prefer. This crust should be baked before filling. If you use pie weights or beans to keep the crust from bubbling during baking (highly recommended), remove the paper and weights for the last few minutes of baking so the crust will brown well.

Preheat the oven to 350°F.

Put the crumbs in a small bowl and stir in the sugar. Pour the melted butter over the crumbs and mix thoroughly. Press the mixture evenly into a 9-inch pie plate.

Bake the empty crust for 8 to 10 minutes, until a dark golden brown (it will continue to harden as it cools). Cool the crust on a wire rack for at least 30 minutes before filling. This crust can be made a day ahead and stored in the refrigerator.

1½ cups fine graham cracker crumbs
¼ cup sugar
6 tablespoons unsalted butter, melted

Mrs. Rowe's Meringue

MAKES ENOUGH TO COVER ONE 9-INCH PIE

Pile this meringue on as thick as you can for a splendid-looking pie. Meringue is a perfect opportunity for the home baker to get creative with the spatula. You can smooth it over, swirl it around, or make fancy peaks. No one way is better than the other. Mrs. Rowe insisted on using a chilled bowl for the mixing. It's a bit of a mystery why, as modern bakers claim it's unnecessary. Maybe her eggs were so fresh that they were still warm and she needed to bring them down to room temperature by using a chilled bowl. In any case, the bakers at Mrs. Rowe's restaurants still use chilled bowls.

Weeping can happen with any meringue. A "weeping" meringue occurs when the sugar solution comes out of the meringue in drops. Sometimes a weeping meringue makes a slimy layer on top of the filling. The meringue will still taste yummy, but it won't be as pretty. Sealing the edges of the meringue is an important step in helping to prevent weeping; it also helps assure that the filling won't spill over. Just add some water to your fingers and press the meringue to the crust along the rim.

4 egg whites, at room temperature

¼ teaspoon cream of tartar

3 tablespoons sugar

Combine the egg whites and cream of tartar in a chilled bowl and beat with an electric mixer on slow to medium speed until soft peaks form. Add the sugar 1 tablespoon at a time and continue beating on slow to medium speed until the whites form stiff peaks but aren't dry. The meringue is now ready to pile lightly over a pie.

Weepless Meringue

Less puffy and showy, but just as delicious as Mrs. Rowe's Meringue (opposite), this family recipe is a tougher breed. The salt and cornstarch fuse and stabilize it, making it easier to manage and giving it a harder glaze once it's baked, which means less likelihood of weeping.

In a saucepan, stir together the cornstarch, 2 tablespoons of the sugar, and enough of the hot water to make a smooth paste. Bring to a simmer over low heat and cook, stirring constantly, until thickened and clear. Set aside to cool.

Combine the egg whites and salt in a chilled bowl and beat with an electric mixer on medium speed until soft peaks form. Add the cooled cornstarch mixture, and then the remaining 6 tablespoons sugar, 1 tablespoon at a time, and continue to beat until the whites form stiff peaks but aren't dry. The meringue is now ready to pile lightly over a pie.

1 tablespoon cornstarch

8 tablespoons sugar

¼ to ½ cup hot water

3 egg whites, at room temperature

Pinch of salt

I'm not sure what "Southern" pie is, but I'll give it some thought. Could it have something to do with blue hair bouffants and lofty meringue?

—JOHN T. EDGE, AUTHOR AND SOUTHERN FOOD EXPERT

Sweetened Whipped Cream

MAKES 1 CUP

If you have never made your own whipped cream, you'll be surprised by how easy it is—and by how much better the flavor is. Soft peaks barely hold together and make a lovely plop on the pie, but the cream doesn't hold up well in this state, so use it quickly. Medium peaks will peak but flop over a bit, and stiff peaks will stand up straight. Stiff is what you want if you are folding it into something else. If you have any left over—most people don't because it's so delicious and easy to eat—it can keep in the refrigerator for a few days in any storage container, but you might have to whisk it a bit before serving.

1 cup heavy cream

1 to 2 tablespoons granulated sugar

1 tablespoon vanilla, optional

Beat the cream with an electric mixer on medium-high speed until frothy and beginning to thicken. Slowly add the sugar in a thin stream. Add the vanilla. Continue whipping until the cream is at the desired consistency.

Caramel Sauce

MAKES 2 CUPS

This sauce is a must for the Layered Ice Cream Pie (page 96), where it meshes with the cookie crust and ice cream for a sinfully delicious combination of textures and flavors. If you're adventurous, this sauce could top off almost any pie.

Combine the butter, sugar, salt, and ¾ cup of the half-and-half in a double boiler. Cook, stirring constantly, until the sugar dissolves, about 10 minutes. Combine the cornstarch and the remaining ¼ cup half-and-half and stir to form a smooth paste. Gradually stir the cornstarch paste into the sugar mixture and continue cooking and stirring until the sauce thickens, about 20 minutes. Stir in the vanilla, then continue to cook, stirring frequently, for 30 minutes. Cool for at least 30 minutes before using.

⅓ cup unsalted butter

1 cup firmly packed brown sugar

⅛ teaspoon salt

1 cup half-and-half

2 teaspoons cornstarch

2 teaspoons vanilla extract

Chocolate Sauce

MAKES 1 CUP

The miniature marshmallows are a great time-saving device in this recipe. Full-size marshmallows also work, but they're more difficult to measure and don't melt as quickly.

1 cup semisweet chocolate chips

⅔ cup miniature marshmallows

1 (5-ounce) can evaporated milk

Combine all of the ingredients in a saucepan over medium heat and cook, stirring frequently, until melted and thoroughly combined, about 6 minutes. Let the mixture cool for at least 20 minutes before using.

CHAPTER 2

Fruit, Berry, and Nut Pies

The fresh pies are so tasty that the locals order slices along with their main courses, just to make sure to get their favorite flavors.

—BILL GOODWIN, *FROMMER'S VIRGINIA*

A TASTE OF APPALACHIAN BOUNTY

Tasting a wild, freshly picked, sun-ripened blackberry is like tasting summer—warm, soft, and sweet, sometimes with a surprising hint of tart. Bake the berries in a pie for summer's sweetest ecstasy.

Throughout Appalachia and the South, wild blackberries, grapes, and blueberries still grow in secret spots passed down through family or friends. The winding hills and fields of Appalachia offer a bountiful harvest of berries, peaches, apples, pears, and grapes, and backyard gardens yield sweet potatoes, pumpkins, and squashes that are as welcome in pie as they are in savory dishes. Throughout the region, Eastern and Southern neighbors share the peanuts that make for delicious peanut and peanut butter pies.

As a child in the earlier part of the twentieth century, Mildred Rowe had access to a premium selection of wild edibles that are hard to find today, like wild grapes, strawberries, blueberries, hazelnuts, and American chestnuts, the latter no longer available because of the blight that wiped out the trees. Mildred learned to read the land, knowing when to check a certain glade of chestnut trees in Rich Patch and what stand of woods offered the best blackberries in Goshen. And she searched for the best apples she could find when she lived in Staunton, where she would become famous for her apple pie and apple dumplings.

Even when it wasn't a survival tactic—as it was when Mildred was a child during the Great Depression—foraging was a lifetime passion for her and her family. Her son Mike says that when he was growing up in Goshen, Virginia, the family often hiked to their favorite spots to pick blackberries. They endured long walks in the blistering heat, nasty poison ivy, and the possibility of running into poisonous snakes or hungry bears in service of finding the juicy little purple nuggets with their tantalizing suggestion of a scrumptious pie or cobbler.

Today, the specialty seasonal pies at Mrs. Rowe's restaurants all use fresh, local ingredients. Regular customers know when to stop by and get a slice of the green tomato mincemeat, strawberry rhubarb, or blackberry pie, and road-smart travelers often plan their trips around Virginia's fruit seasons and Mrs. Rowe's pies. A piece of seasonal pie offers more than a taste of home for travel-weary eaters; they're also sampling authentic local traditions and the season in each and every bite.

Apple-Dapple Pie

MAKES TWO 9-INCH PIES

This moist and crumbly pie has a consistency almost like a coffee cake. As a result, unlike most pies, it's safe to cut into this one when it's slightly warm. As with all prebaked pastry crusts, it's important to cover the edges with foil or crust shields while the filling bakes, so it doesn't burn. Walnuts, almonds, or pecans work nicely with this pie.

Preheat the oven to 350°F.

Beat the eggs, sugar, oil, and vanilla in a large bowl until thoroughly combined. Add the flour, baking soda, cinnamon, and salt and mix thoroughly. Stir in the apples and nuts until evenly combined, then spoon the mixture into the 2 crusts.

Bake for 45 to 50 minutes, until a toothpick inserted in the center comes out almost clean, then transfer to wire racks to cool.

As soon as the pies are out of the oven, prepare the topping by mixing the butter, sugar, and milk in a small bowl until thoroughly combined. After the pies have cooled for about 10 minutes, pour ¾ of the topping over the pies, then cool the pies completely (for about 1 hour), or enjoy them warm. Serve the leftover topping on the side for people who want extra on their slice.

1 recipe Plain Pie Pastry (page 17) or Vinegar Pie Crust (page 19), prebaked

3 eggs

2 cups sugar

1½ cups light vegetable oil

1 teaspoon vanilla extract

3 cups all-purpose flour

1 teaspoon baking soda

1 teaspoon ground cinnamon

1 teaspoon salt

3 cups diced apples

1 cup chopped raw or toasted nuts

TOPPING

½ cup unsalted butter, melted

1 cup brown sugar

¼ cup whole milk

French Apple Pie

MAKES ONE 9-INCH PIE

This pie offers a perfect blend of apples and raisins. You can add the sweet icing, which is a surprising and delightful touch—or a scoop of vanilla ice cream on a blisteringly hot, Southern summer day.

To make the raisin filling, combine the raisins, water, and lemon juice in a heavy saucepan over medium heat. Bring to a boil, then lower the heat to medium-low and cook, stirring occasionally until the raisins are plump, about 15 minutes.

Separately, combine the corn syrup, flour, and sugar and mix well, then add to the raisins and continue cooking, stirring occasionally, until thick and syrupy, about 10 minutes. Remove from the heat and cool until the mixture is just warm, about 10 to 15 minutes.

Preheat the oven to 400°F. Line a 9-inch pie plate with 1 rolled-out crust.

Peel the apples, cut them into thin wedges, and put them in a large bowl. Separately, combine the sugars, cinnamon, nutmeg, and cornstarch, then add to the apples and gently stir until evenly mixed.

(continued)

1 recipe Plain Pie Pastry (page 17) or Vinegar Pie Crust (page 19)

RAISIN FILLING

⅔ cup raisins

6 tablespoons water

½ teaspoon lemon juice

¼ cup light corn syrup

1½ teaspoons all-purpose flour

1½ teaspoons sugar

2 apples (preferably a tart variety)

¼ cup brown sugar

½ cup sugar

¼ teaspoon ground cinnamon

½ teaspoon ground nutmeg

1½ teaspoons cornstarch

ICING

1 cup confectioners' sugar

2 tablespoons water

1 tablespoon butter, softened

French Apple Pie, continued

Spread the apple mixture in the crust in an even layer, then spread the raisin filling evenly over the apples. Brush the rim of the crust with water, cover with the second rolled-out crust, seal and flute or crimp the edges, and cut a steam vent in the center.

Bake for 40 to 50 minutes, until golden brown. Cool on a wire rack for 1 to 2 hours, until completely cool.

To make the icing, combine the sugar and water and mix well. Add the butter and mix until smooth. Brush over the top of the cooled pie before serving.

In January of 2008, *Family Circle* magazine reported that Americans' favorite pie is the apple pie. Next are pumpkin, cherry, and lemon meringue, with chocolate and pecan tied for fifth place.

Caramel Apple Nut Pie

MAKES ONE 9-INCH PIE

This pretty pie is reminiscent of the toffee apples that were a fairground favorite in Mrs. Rowe's day. The brown sugar delivers a gooey, sweet flavor. For an extra treat, serve with a scoop of cinnamon ice cream.

Preheat the oven to 400°F. Line a 9-inch pie plate with 1 rolled-out crust.

Put the brown sugar, flour, salt, and cream in a small bowl and stir until thoroughly combined, then stir in the nuts. Put the apples in a large bowl and add the sugar mixture. The mixture will be very thick, so it's easier to use your hands to do the mixing.

Spread the apples evenly in the crust, then scatter the butter over the top. Brush the rim of the crust with water, cover with the second rolled-out crust, seal and flute or crimp the edges, and cut a few steam vents in the top. Brush the top crust with the milk, then sprinkle with a bit of sugar.

Bake for about 40 to 45 minutes, until the crust is golden brown and the fruit is tender. Cool on a wire rack for 1 to 2 hours before slicing. Serve at room temperature or slightly warm.

1 recipe Plain Pie Pastry (page 17) or Vinegar Pie Crust (page 19)

¾ cup firmly packed brown sugar

3 tablespoons all-purpose flour

Pinch of salt

¼ cup heavy cream

1 cup chopped walnuts or pecans

6 cups peeled, sliced apples, preferably McIntosh or Granny Smith (4 or 5 apples)

3 tablespoons cold unsalted butter, cut into bits

1 tablespoon whole milk or cream

Brown, granulated, or raw sugar, for sprinkling

Crabapple Pie

MAKES ONE 9-INCH PIE

Crabapples grow abundantly in Appalachia and in other parts of the South. It takes a lot of these small apples to make 6 cups, but for people who love tart apples, this tiny power-house of a fruit is unbeatable. Depending on where you live, the season starts in August and sometimes continues into early winter. Whenever crabapple season occurs in your area, make it a point to slip this unusual treat into your yearly pie rituals. To core the crabapples, slice off the blossom end with a paring knife and cut around the core in four cuts. This will leave a squarish core, which is much easier than trying to halve and core the crabapples. If you can't find crabapples, substitute tart apples, such as Granny Smith, and coat the diced apples with the vanilla, lemon juice, and water right away, instead of sprinkling them on after the pie is filled.

1 recipe Plain Pie Pastry (page 17) or Vinegar Pie Crust (page 19)

6 cups cored and finely chopped red crabapples, peels left on

1 cup sugar

1 tablespoon all-purpose flour

¼ teaspoon salt

1 teaspoon vanilla extract

1½ tablespoons lemon juice

¼ cup water

1 tablespoon whole milk or cream

Brown, granulated, or raw sugar, for sprinkling

Preheat the oven to 450°F. Line a 9-inch pie plate with 1 rolled-out crust.

Toss the crabapples with the sugar, flour, and salt. Spread the filling in the crust, then sprinkle with the vanilla, lemon juice, and water. Brush the rim of the crust with water, cover with the second rolled-out crust, seal and flute or crimp the edges, and cut a few steam vents in the top. Brush the top crust with the milk, then sprinkle with the sugar.

Bake for 10 minutes, then lower the oven temperature to 375°F and bake another 40 to 45 minutes, until golden brown and bubbling. Cool on a wire rack for 1 to 2 hours before slicing. Serve at room temperature or slightly warm.

Granny Smith Apple Pie

MAKES ONE 9-INCH PIE

If you like the flavor of sour apples, cut the amount of sugar in the filling to ⅓ cup. If you want to enhance the sweetness, serve with a scoop of vanilla or cinnamon ice cream. This recipe comes from Cynthia Craig, a longtime baker at the restaurant.

Preheat the oven to 425°F. Line a 9-inch pie plate with 1 rolled-out crust.

Put the apples in a large bowl, add the lemon juice, and toss to coat. Separately, combine the sugar, flour, cinnamon, and nutmeg, mix thoroughly, then add to the apples. Gently stir until the apples are thoroughly coated, then spoon the mixture evenly into the crust. Dot the top with the butter.

Brush the rim of the crust with water, cover with the second rolled-out crust, seal and flute or crimp the edges, and cut a few steam vents in the top.

To make the glaze, mix the warm milk with the sugar. Brush the glaze over the top crust.

Bake for 15 minutes, then lower the oven temperature to 350°F and bake another 30 to 40 minutes, until the crust is golden brown and the fruit is tender. Check the pie about halfway through the baking time, and if the edges of the crust are getting too brown, cover them with pie shields or foil. Cool on a wire rack for 1 to 2 hours before slicing. Serve at room temperature or slightly warm.

1 recipe Plain Pie Pastry (page 17)
   or Vinegar Pie Crust (page 19)

6 cups peeled and sliced Granny Smith or other tart apples (about 2 pounds)

1 tablespoon lemon juice

½ cup packed brown sugar

3 tablespoons all-purpose flour

¾ teaspoon ground cinnamon

¼ teaspoon ground nutmeg

1 tablespoon unsalted butter, cut into bits

GLAZE

1 tablespoon warm whole milk

1 teaspoon sugar

Fresh Peach Pie

MAKES ONE 9-INCH PIE

Peach season is fleeting, but this seasonal pie is so delicious that you should slip it into your summer any way you can. If the edges of the crust begin to brown before the rest of the pie, cover them with foil. Enjoy plain or add a scoop of vanilla ice cream.

1 recipe Plain Pie Pastry (page 17)
  or Vinegar Pie Crust (page 19)

5 cups peeled and sliced fresh peaches

1½ teaspoons lemon juice

1 cup sugar

¼ cup all-purpose flour

½ teaspoon ground cinnamon

⅛ teaspoon ground nutmeg

2 tablespoons unsalted butter, melted

Preheat the oven to 425°F. Line a 9-inch pie plate with 1 rolled-out crust.

Put the peaches in a bowl, add the lemon juice, and gently stir to coat. Separately, combine the sugar, flour, cinnamon, and nutmeg, mix thoroughly, then add to the peaches. Gently stir to coat the peaches, then spoon the filling evenly into the crust.

Brush the rim of the crust with water, cover with the second rolled-out crust, seal and flute or crimp the edges, and cut a few steam vents in the top.

Bake for 35 to 40 minutes, until golden brown. Remove from the oven, brush with the melted butter, and cool on a wire rack for 1 hour before slicing. Serve at room temperature or slightly warm.

Mrs. Brown's Grape Pie

MAKES ONE 9-INCH PIE

Eric Brown, an employee at Mrs. Rowe's Restaurant and Bakery for eleven years, asked his mother for his favorite grape pie recipe and she graciously offered it to us—for all true pie lovers and bakers are generous in spirit and love to share recipes. When Mildred Rowe was a child, she often picked wild grapes, which used to grow plentifully in the Appalachians. "Mother told us how they fought the wild turkeys for the grapes," says Mike DiGrassie. This recipe calls for Concord grapes since many of us don't live near a wild grape patch. It's one of the few grape pie recipes that doesn't require peeling the grapes.

½ recipe Plain Pie Pastry (page 17) or Vinegar Pie Crust (page 19), prebaked

4 cups fresh Concord grapes, washed and stems removed

2 cups water

1 cup sugar

½ cup plus 2 tablespoons cornstarch

Sweetened Whipped Cream (page 26), for topping

Combine the grapes and water in a large saucepan over high heat and bring to a boil. Lower the heat to medium and cook until the fruit is very soft and the liquid is dark, about 10 minutes.

Strain the juice into a bowl, pressing the grapes with the back of a spoon to extract as much juice as possible. Let the juice cool until lukewarm, then pour it back into the saucepan and place over high heat.

Whisk the sugar and cornstarch together, then pour the mixture into the grape juice and whisk until thoroughly combined. Bring to a boil and continue whisking frequently until thickened. Boil for at least 1 full minute to reduce the cornstarch taste. The mixture should be smooth and very thick.

Pour the filling into the crust and chill for 2 to 3 hours before slicing. Serve topped with a dollop of whipped cream.

Damson Plum Pie

MAKES ONE 9-INCH PIE

Damson plums were first introduced to the British by the Romans, and eventually English settlers brought them over to America, where they thrived in the climate of the eastern United States. Because of their acidic, tart flavor, Damsons make tasty jams and pies. This recipe, handwritten by Mildred in one of her old notebooks, calls for Damson plums—if you substitute another variety of plum, you may need to cut back on the sugar.

Preheat the oven to 425°F. Line a 9-inch pie plate with 1 rolled-out crust.

Put the plums in a bowl, add the lemon juice, and gently stir to coat. Add the sugar and flour, mix lightly, then spread the filling in the crust. Scatter the butter over the filling. Brush the rim of the crust with water, cover with the second rolled-out crust, seal and flute or crimp the edges, and cut a few steam vents in the top.

Bake at 425°F for 40 minutes, then lower the oven temperature to 350°F and bake another 20 to 30 minutes, until the crust is golden brown and the fruit is tender. Cool on a wire rack for 1 to 2 hours before slicing and serve at room temperature.

Variation: If you like, you can substitute a crumb topping for the top crust. Just sift together ¾ cup flour and ½ cup sugar, then add ⅓ cup butter and cut it in until crumbly. Sprinkle over the fruit filling before baking the pie.

1 recipe Plain Pie Pastry (page 17) or Vinegar Pie Crust (page 19)

2 cups sliced Damson plums

1 teaspoon lemon juice

1⅓ cups sugar

5 tablespoons all-purpose flour

1 tablespoon cold unsalted butter, cut into bits

Blueberry Pie

MAKES ONE 9-INCH PIE

Mike DiGrassie recalls, "We used to have blueberries growing all over our camp. The birds went crazy over them. When I tried picking some for myself there was always some bird eyeballin' me." Due to the high cost of blueberries, this is the most expensive whole pie at Mrs. Rowe's—but you can still get a deep blue slice for the regular price of $2.75.

1 recipe Plain Pie Pastry (page 17)
   or Vinegar Pie Crust (page 19)

6 cups blueberries, fresh or frozen
   (thawed and drained if frozen)

2 tablespoons lemon juice

½ cup sugar

¼ cup all-purpose flour

¾ teaspoon ground cinnamon

2 tablespoons cold unsalted butter, cut
   into bits

1 egg beaten with 1 tablespoon whole
   milk, for egg wash

Line a 9-inch pie plate with 1 rolled-out crust and place in the refrigerator to chill.

Put the blueberries in a bowl, add the lemon juice, and stir to coat. Separately, combine the sugar, flour, and cinnamon, mix thoroughly, and then stir into the blueberries. Spread the filling in the crust, and scatter the butter over the top. Brush the rim of the crust with the egg wash, cover with the second rolled-out crust, and seal and flute or crimp the edges.

Put the pie in the refrigerator to chill until firm, about 30 minutes. Store the remaining egg wash in the refrigerator too. Preheat the oven to 425°F.

Brush the top crust with egg wash, then score the top with 2 perpendicular cuts for steam vents. Bake for 20 minutes, then lower the oven temperature to 350°F and bake for another 30 to 40 minutes, until the juices are bubbling and the crust is golden brown. Cool on a wire rack for at least 2 hours before slicing, then chill in the refrigerator until ready to serve. Serve chilled or warm.

Strawberry Pie

MAKES TWO 9-INCH PIES

On Mother's Day, 2008, Mrs. Rowe's Country Buffet sold out of its fifty-six strawberry pies—it's become such an integral part of the local tradition. You must use fresh berries for this pie. Frozen ones would make the pie too runny. For variety, you can use any kind of fresh berry; just make sure the berry and the flavor of gelatin complement one another.

Combine the water, sugar, gelatin, and cornstarch in a saucepan over medium-high heat and cook, whisking constantly, until thickened. The mixture should feel thick and thinly coat a spoon, and a line drawn on the spoon will stay clear. Cool until lukewarm.

Place the strawberries in the crust pointed end up, starting in the middle and working out to the edge. Pour half of the gelatin mixture over the strawberries in each pie shell.

Chill for several hours or overnight, until the filling is set. Serve topped with a dollop of whipped topping.

1 recipe Plain Pie Pastry (page 17) or Vinegar Pie Crust (page 19), prebaked

1½ cups water

1½ cups sugar

1 (3-ounce) package strawberry gelatin

3 tablespoons cornstarch

2 pounds fresh strawberries, washed and hulled

Whipped topping or Sweetened Whipped Cream (page 26), for topping

Blackberry Pie

MAKES ONE 9-INCH PIE

If you have access to a bramble of blackberry bushes, guard it with your life. The price of blackberries makes it more than reasonable to pick your own, besides which nothing is quite so satisfying as picking your own berries. Perhaps it's knowing where the food came from and taking part in the ancient practice of foraging. If you must use frozen berries, you should measure them while they're still frozen, because they shrivel as they thaw. Also, it's important to thaw and drain frozen berries before placing them in the pie shell, otherwise the pie will be watery. Use potato starch in this pie if you can. It gives the filling a clear, jewel-like color, and it has less flavor than cornstarch.

Whisk the potato starch and sugar together and set aside. Put 1 cup of the berries in a small saucepan and mash them with a fork. Cook and stir over medium heat for about 7 minutes, until the berries begin to break down and release their juice. Stir the cornstarch mixture into the berries and cook and stir until thick and bubbling and the sugar is dissolved, about 7 minutes. The mixture should coat a spoon and a line drawn along the spoon will stay clear. Cool until lukewarm.

Spread the remaining berries in the crust, then pour the cooked mixture over the berries and gently stir until evenly distributed.

Chill for 3 to 4 hours or overnight, until the filling is set. Serve garnished with a dollop of whipped cream.

½ recipe Plain Pie Pastry (page 17) or Vinegar Pie Crust (page 19), prebaked

3 tablespoons cornstarch or potato starch

1 cup sugar

4½ cups blackberries

Sweetened Whipped Cream (page 26), for topping

Gooseberry Pie

MAKES ONE 9-INCH PIE

This pie recipe is shared by Susan Simmons, a baker at Mrs. Rowe's Catering. Although most people consider the gooseberry to be a British fruit, it also flourishes in the eastern United States. The flavor of this pie is a wonderful balance of tart and sweet, with the perfect touch of cinnamon. This pie comes out flat, not mounded, but packs a powerful flavor. Serve with a scoop of vanilla ice cream for a delicious play of texture.

1 recipe Plain Pie Pastry (page 17) or Vinegar Pie Crust (page 19)

¼ cup crisp rice cereal

¾ cup sugar, plus additional for sprinkling

2 tablespoons all-purpose flour

1 tablespoon cornstarch

Pinch of salt

⅛ teaspoon ground cinnamon

2 cups gooseberries, fresh, frozen, or canned

1 tablespoon cold unsalted butter, cut into bits

1 egg beaten with 1 tablespoon whole milk, for egg wash

Preheat the oven to 425°F. Line a 9-inch pie plate with 1 rolled-out crust, then sprinkle the cereal in the crust in an even layer. (This will keep the bottom crust from getting soggy.)

Put the sugar, flour, cornstarch, salt, and cinnamon in a bowl and stir to combine. Drain the berries if using canned, then stir the berries into the sugar mixture. Spread the filling evenly in the crust, then scatter the butter over the top.

Brush the rim of the crust with the egg wash, cover with the second rolled-out crust, seal and flute or crimp the edges, and cut a few steam vents in the top. Brush the top crust with egg wash and sprinkle with a bit of sugar.

Bake for 15 minutes, then lower the oven temperature to 350°F and bake for another 30 minutes, until golden brown. Cool on a wire rack for 1 to 2 hours before slicing. Serve at room temperature.

Simple Cherry Pie

MAKES ONE 9-INCH PIE

This recipe was found in one of Mrs. Rowe's old handwritten notebooks. You can substitute fresh cherries or, for a special treat, use fresh sour cherries. You may want to adjust how much sugar you use, based on the sweetness of the cherries.

Preheat the oven to 350°F. Line a 9-inch pie plate with 1 rolled-out crust.

Mix the cornstarch with ¼ cup of the water to form a smooth paste. Put the cherries in a saucepan over medium-high heat, stir in the sugar and the remaining ¼ cup water, and bring to a boil. Lower the heat to medium, stir in the cornstarch, and cook, stirring constantly, until thick, about 5 minutes.

Sprinkle the flour in the bottom of the prepared pie crust, then pour in the cherry filling and spread it out evenly.

Bake for 45 minutes, until the crust is golden brown. Cool on a wire rack for about 2 hours before slicing. Serve at room temperature.

½ recipe Plain Pie Pastry (page 17) or Vinegar Pie Crust (page 19)

3 tablespoons cornstarch

½ cup water

1 (16-ounce) can cherries, tart or sweet

1½ cups sugar

2 tablespoons all-purpose flour

Spicy Pumpkin Pie

MAKES ONE 10-INCH PIE

This pie, so deep orange that it's almost brown, gives off a heavenly scent as it bakes. It's a warmer, richer twist on the traditional pumpkin pie recipe. If you like, garnish the center of the pie with pecans after it's baked.

½ recipe Plain Pie Pastry (page 17)
    or Vinegar Pie Crust (page 19)

1 (15-ounce) can pumpkin

½ cup packed brown sugar

1 tablespoon dark molasses

½ teaspoon salt

1½ teaspoons ground cinnamon

¼ teaspoon ground cloves

2 eggs, slightly beaten

1 cup half-and-half, scalded

½ cup Sweetened Whipped Cream
    (page 26), for topping

Preheat the oven to 400°F. Line a 10-inch pie plate with the rolled-out crust.

Put the pumpkin, sugar, molasses, salt, cinnamon, cloves, and eggs in a bowl and stir until thoroughly combined. Gradually stir in the half-and-half, then pour the filling into the crust.

Bake for 10 minutes, then lower the oven temperature to 350°F and bake another 30 to 40 minutes, until the center of the filling is firm. Cool on wire rack for 1 to 2 hours. Spoon the whipped cream in a ring around the outer edge of the filling before slicing and serving.

Sweet Potato Pie

MAKE ONE 9-INCH PIE

Mildred's grandson Aaron DiGrassie learned to make this pie during his days of cooking at the Excelsior Hotel in Italy. With its sturdy texture and perfect amount of sweetness, this recipe seems like it could have come from any Southern granny's recipe file.

Preheat the oven to 400°F. Line a 9-inch pie plate with the rolled-out crust.

Place the potatoes into a saucepan and add water. Cover and boil gently 20 minutes or until tender. The water should be almost evaporated. Drain off any remaining water. Mash with a mixer until smooth.

Whip the eggs in a bowl until frothy. Add the sweet potatoes, sugar, cinnamon, nutmeg, cloves, milk, butter, and salt and mix until smooth. Pour the filling into the crust.

Bake for 20 minutes, then lower the oven temperature to 375°F and bake another 15 to 20 minutes, until almost completely set. The filling should wobble very slightly in the center when the pan is jiggled, but a toothpick inserted 1 inch from the edge should come out clean. Cool on a wire rack for 1 to 2 hours before slicing. Serve at room temperature.

½ recipe Plain Pie Pastry (page 17) or Vinegar Pie Crust (page 19)

4 to 5 medium sweet potatoes (2¼ cups mashed and cooked)

3 eggs

½ cup brown sugar

1 teaspoon ground cinnamon

½ teaspoon ground nutmeg

¼ teaspoon ground cloves

1⅓ cups whole milk

1½ teaspoons unsalted butter, melted

⅛ teaspoon salt

Butternut Squash Pie

MAKES ONE 10-INCH PIE

This extremely moist pie tastes milky and sweet. The consistency is nothing like pumpkin pie; rather than being a smooth custard, it's sturdy and textured.

½ recipe Plain Pie Pastry (page 17)
　　or Vinegar Pie Crust (page 19)

1 pound butternut squash

1 cup white sugar

½ teaspoon ground ginger

¼ teaspoon ground cinnamon

⅛ teaspoon ground nutmeg

Pinch of salt

1½ cups hot whole milk

2 eggs

1 egg yolk

1 tablespoon unsalted butter, melted

Preheat the oven to 400°F. Lightly grease a baking sheet or 9 by 13-inch baking pan or line it with foil.

Cut the squash in half lengthwise, scoop out the seeds, and place on the baking sheet cut-side down. Bake for about 30 minutes, until tender. Once the squash is cool enough to handle, scoop the flesh into a bowl and mash it. Measure out 2 cups of squash and refrigerate any leftovers for another use.

Turn the oven up to 425°F. Line a 10-inch pie plate with the rolled-out crust.

Put the sugar, ginger, cinnamon, nutmeg, and salt in a bowl and stir to combine. Blend in the milk, squash, eggs, egg yolk, and butter. Pour the filling into the crust, just to the top of the crust; discard any extra filling, or pour it into a small greased custard cup and bake it alongside the pie (it will probably be done sooner than the pie).

Bake for 50 to 60 minutes, or until almost completely set. The filling should wobble very slightly in the center when the pan is jiggled, but a knife inserted in the center should come out clean. Check the crust halfway through the baking time; it will probably need pie shields or foil to prevent overbrowning. Cool on a wire rack 1 to 2 hours before slicing. Serve at room temperature.

The more I study the distinct regions of the South and their foodways, the more obvious it becomes that people used what would grow in their area. That is reflected in the fruit/vegetable pies as well as other dishes people prepared.

—LORNA REEVES, EDITOR, *TASTE OF THE SOUTH* MAGAZINE

Mrs. Brown's Winter Squash Pie

MAKES ONE 9-INCH PIE

Thanks to Mrs. Brown, mother of longtime Mrs. Rowe's employee Eric Brown, for this gently flavored pie recipe. It's a testament to the Southern creative ability to use everything from the garden, not letting anything go to waste.

½ recipe Plain Pie Pastry (page 17)
   or Vinegar Pie Crust (page 19)

½ pound pureed cooked acorn or
   butternut squash

2 cups whole milk

½ cup sugar

2 tablespoons all-purpose flour

1 teaspoon pumpkin pie spice

⅛ teaspoon salt

2 eggs, beaten

1½ teaspoons vanilla extract

Ground nutmeg, for sprinkling

Preheat the oven to 350°F. Line a 9-inch pie plate with the rolled-out crust.

Cut the squash in half lengthwise, scoop out the seeds, and place on the baking sheet cut-side down. Bake for about 30 minutes, until tender. Once the squash is cool enough to handle, scoop the flesh into a bowl and mash it. Measure out 1 cup of squash and refrigerate any leftovers for another use.

Put the milk in a saucepan over medium high heat and stir in the squash. Cook, stirring occasionally, just until the milk is steaming. Remove from the heat and stir in the sugar, flour, pumpkin pie spice, and salt, then add the eggs and vanilla and stir until thoroughly combined. Pour the filling into the crust and sprinkle with a bit of nutmeg.

Bake for about 45 minutes, until set in the center. A toothpick inserted 1 inch from the edge should come out clean and the center should have a slight shimmer. Cool on a wire rack for 1 to 2 hours before slicing. Serve slightly warm or cool.

Chestnut Pie

MAKES ONE 9-INCH PIE

When she was a child, Mildred harvested and sold chestnuts. She often arose earlier in the morning than her brothers and sisters to pick the cherished nuts, which were a cash crop for many Appalachian families. But by 1950, most American Chestnut trees were wiped out by a devastating blight. Even though you can't pick chestnuts from a tree growing in the forest now, you can certainly buy chestnuts in the grocery store—most of which aren't grown in the United States. Processing chestnuts isn't a chore to be taken lightly because of their very hard shells, so we recommend using sweetened chestnut puree, which can be found in better grocery stores. This pie is moist and has a pleasant hint of orange flavor to complement the earthy, sweet chestnut taste.

Preheat the oven to 350°F. Line a 9-inch pie plate with the rolled-out crust.

Whisk the egg yolks in a bowl, then add the chestnut puree, cream, sugar, orange juice, and Grand Marnier. Beat with the whisk until entirely smooth, then fold in the egg whites. Spread the filling evenly in the crust, then sprinkle with the nutmeg.

Bake for 45 to 50 minutes, until center is set and a knife inserted in the center comes out clean. Cool on wire rack for 1 hour, then chill for at least 1 hour before slicing. Serve cold, topped with a dollop of whipped cream.

½ recipe Plain Pie Pastry (page 17) or Vinegar Pie Crust (page 19)

3 egg yolks

1½ cups (about 1 pound) sweetened chestnut puree

1 cup heavy cream

½ cup sugar

1 tablespoon orange juice

1 tablespoon Grand Marnier

2 egg whites, beaten until stiff

Ground nutmeg, for sprinkling

Sweetened Whipped Cream (page 26), for topping

Hickory Nut Pie

MAKES ONE 9-INCH PIE

Hickory nuts are only available in a few areas of the country, and the South is one of them. They're usually sold in their shells, which are extremely thick and hard. But if you're a hickory nut lover, this pie will inspire you to do the hard work of shelling them. If you can't find hickory nuts, pecans are in the hickory family and make a great substitute. A shot of bourbon enhances the flavor—and makes it even more Southern. For a crisp bottom crust, parbake the shell before filling it. For a crunchy pie, go with the larger amount of nuts.

Preheat the oven to 325°F. Line a 9-inch pie plate with the rolled-out crust and pour the nuts into the crust.

Combine the corn syrup, butter, and sugar in a saucepan over low heat and cook, stirring constantly, until sugar is entirely dissolved, about 15 to 20 minutes. Cool for about 10 minutes.

Beat the eggs, vanilla, and salt in a small bowl, then add to the sugar mixture and beat well. Spread the filling evenly in the crust.

Bake for 50 to 55 minutes, until the center is set and doesn't jiggle when the pan is tapped. Cool on wire rack for at least 30 minutes before slicing. This pie can be served warm or cold.

½ recipe Plain Pie Pastry (page 17) or Vinegar Pie Crust (page 19)

1 to 1½ cups hickory nuts or pecans, broken

1 cup light corn syrup

½ cup unsalted butter, melted

1 cup sugar

4 eggs, beaten

1 teaspoon vanilla extract

½ teaspoon salt

Mincemeat Pie

MAKES ONE 9-INCH DEEP-DISH PIE

Bonnie Cash, a customer at Mrs. Rowe's, says, "When my husband used to travel on business and was in Staunton, he always ate lunch or dinner at Rowe's. He ate there so often that on one occasion Mildred told him she wanted to cook dinner for him and invited him home to eat. He would never eat mincemeat pie. Well, she served mincemeat pie and he ate it so as not to disappoint her. It turns out that it is also now a favorite during the holidays. I must admit he never had eaten 'real' mincemeat before." This mincemeat is about as "real" as it gets. According to Grace Firth in her book Stillroom Cookery: The Art of Preserving Foods Naturally, *"Mincemeat is a salute to the triumph of nature and humanity's ingenuity in bringing it all together in pie." Because making mincemeat is an undertaking, make a huge batch of it, keep it in the refrigerator, and make fresh pies all season long.*

1 recipe Plain Pie Pastry (page 17)
  or Vinegar Pie Crust (page 19)
2½ cups Mincemeat (recipe follows)
2 tablespoons unsalted butter, melted

Preheat the oven to 375°F. Line a 9-inch deep-dish pie plate with 1 rolled-out crust.

Spread the mincemeat evenly in the crust, then cover with the second rolled-out crust. Seal the edges, and cut several steam vents in the top.

Bake for 35 to 40 minutes, until the crust is golden brown. Remove from the oven, brush with the melted butter, and cool on a wire rack for about 2 hours before slicing. Serve at room temperature.

Season the beef with the salt and pepper, then put it in a large pot over medium-low heat, cover with water, and simmer for about 45 minutes, until tender.

Once the beef has cooled, coarsely grind it, along with the suet, apples, and citron. Transfer to a large bowl and stir in the raisins, currants, brown sugar, cider, cinnamon, nutmeg, cloves, allspice, and lemon juice. Tightly pack the mincemeat into sterilized jars and refrigerate for at least 4 weeks before using. It will keep up to 6 weeks in the refrigerator.

MINCEMEAT (makes about 12 cups)

1 pound lean beef chunks

1½ teaspoons salt

1½ teaspoons ground black pepper

8 ounces beef suet

2½ pounds York or Stayman apples, peeled, cored, and sliced

4 ounces candied citron

3½ cups seedless raisins

3¼ cups currants

2¼ cups packed brown sugar

3 cups apple cider

1 tablespoon ground cinnamon

1½ teaspoons ground nutmeg

1½ teaspoons ground cloves

1½ teaspoons ground allspice

Juice of 1 lemon

Green Tomato Mincemeat Pie

MAKES ONE 10-INCH PIE

There are never any leftovers of this flavorful pie at Mrs. Rowe's Country Buffet. Because green tomatoes have such a short season, customers have many long months to look forward to this pie, with its robust spice and vinegar essences perfectly mingled with an underlying sweetness. The flavors unfold with every bite. Longtime regular customers know to get to the restaurant early enough to enjoy a slice. If the green tomato season slips by, try tomatillos instead. This pie also works as a side dish with pork chops or chicken.

1 recipe Plain Pie Pastry (page 17) or Vinegar Pie Crust (page 19)

1½ pounds green tomatoes or tomatillos

½ tablespoon salt

1¾ pounds apples

2¼ cups packed brown sugar

2¾ cups seedless raisins

1 tablespoon plus ¾ teaspoon ground cinnamon

1 teaspoon ground allspice

1½ teaspoons ground nutmeg

1½ tablespoons lemon juice

½ cup plus 2 tablespoons white or apple cider vinegar

Grind the tomatoes using a food processor or food mill until they are a roughly textured consistency (this is mock mincemeat, after all!). Put the tomatoes in a large nonreactive saucepan, add the salt, and let stand for 1 hour.

Drain the tomatoes, return them to the saucepan, and add water to cover. Place over high heat and bring to a boil and cook, stirring occasionally for 5 minutes, then drain and return to the saucepan.

Peel, core, and finely chop the apples. Add them to the tomatoes, then stir in the sugar, raisins, cinnamon, allspice, nutmeg, lemon juice, and vinegar. Place over high heat, mix thoroughly, and bring to a boil. Turn down the heat as low as possible and simmer for 1 hour, stirring frequently to prevent the bottom from burning.

Cool to room temperature, which could take as long as 1½ hours. The filling will keep in the refrigerator for 7 to 10 days and also freezes well, if you'd like to make it in advance or make extra to enjoy once green tomato season has ended.

Preheat the oven to 425°F. Line a 10-inch pie plate with 1 rolled-out crust.

Spread the filling evenly in the crust, then cover with the second rolled-out crust. Seal and flute or crimp the edges and cut a few steam vents in the top.

Bake for 15 minutes, then lower the oven temperature to 350°F and continue to bake until the crust takes on a golden hue, about 35 minutes. Cool on a wire rack for 2 hours before slicing. Serve at room temperature or cold.

CHAPTER 3

Cream and Custard Pies

Many times throughout the years, we traveled to see my granny in West Virginia and passed right through Staunton, and every time we would stop and have lunch at Mrs. Rowe's. When I was a little girl, I would count the miles until we got there—just craving a piece of her chocolate pie. Yum.

—KENDRA BAILEY MORRIS, "ACCIDENTAL CHEF"
COLUMNIST, *RICHMOND TIMES DISPATCH*

SLICES OF SERENITY

The most popular pie at Mrs. Rowe's Restaurant and Bakery—the Original Coconut Cream Pie (page 64)—was one that Mildred learned to make in the sleepy village of Goshen, Virginia, as a new restaurant owner in 1947. She fell in love with the creamy pie that tasted of tropical coconut—a new flavor to her Appalachian palate. She mastered the pie in her own kitchen and spread the joy of it to her family and loyal customers.

Imagine traveling Virginia's dusty, bumpy country roads before the days of interstates and superhighways in the 1940s and 1950s—a time actually not so long ago. Most road food wasn't appetizing, so many families traveled with their own food. Mrs. Rowe's Restaurant and Bakery, first in Goshen, then in Staunton, beckoned with a welcoming homemade meal topped off with a slice of comforting, creamy, sweet pie—a touch of home for road-weary travelers, or for locals with a hankering for good pie.

Customers would sometimes even plan their road trips around a stop at the restaurant. Customer Bonnie Cash says, "Our favorite pie is and has always been Mildred's egg custard pie. The one thing about egg custard pie is that they only made it on Tuesdays, so we would plan our trips to Staunton on a Tuesday just to get a slice of egg custard pie! Oftentimes we even called ahead to make sure it was on the menu and asked them to save us some." You can find the recipe for this old-fashioned pie in *Mrs. Rowe's Restaurant Cookbook*.

The most popular pie at Mrs. Rowe's Country Buffet, peanut butter pie, is also cream based. Like the egg custard, this pie recipe can be found in *Mrs. Rowe's Restaurant Cookbook*—but this chapter showcases two variations, Smoothest Ever Peanut Butter Pie (page 82) and Peanut Butter Custard Pie (page 83). At the Mount Crawford eatery, full-time baker Angie Bedlinsky, born in Ukraine and now a proud new American citizen, stirs huge double boilers, one containing peanut butter filling and the other filled with smooth, canary yellow lemon filling. The smells of the two combine in a heavenly swoon with the egg custard pies baking in one of the four ovens. Steam floats from the pies as she pours the thick liquid into the crusts.

A robust, hardworking woman whose hands have a light, butterfly-like grace, Angie flits between stirring cream fillings as they cook, checking on the egg custard pies in the ovens, and slicing finished and cooled pies, which she expertly scoops onto tiny pie plates situated on trays to be carried to the pie bar. Angie usually makes between sixty and seventy pies a day (this count doesn't include specialty pies for holidays) and she says softly, with a smile, and without a trace of bravado, "Usually I don't make mistakes."

"Now, I *have* made some mistakes," says Cynthia Craig, a baker at Mrs. Rowe's Restaurant for eight years, but an employee for twenty-one. Her mother, Juanita Chittum, is also a longtime employee. But Cynthia doesn't only craft pies and rolls, like Angie. She also makes bread, biscuits, and sweet rolls for breakfast. "The difference is the buffet doesn't serve breakfast, so all Angie does is the pie and rolls, which is enough because of the volume of pie they go through." Cynthia's day begins at two or three o'clock in the morning and usually ends with making the cream pies in the midmorning.

Both bakers are exacting in their use of every bit of the ingredients. Glancing into the double boilers at Mrs. Rowe's Country Buffet, not even one drop of luscious pie filling is left for eager fingers longing to sneak just one little taste.

[Mrs. Rowe's Country Buffet] always has an amazing assortment of pie. It is hard to choose because there are so many good ones and many old-time favorites that are not usually found at most restaurants. It tempts you to try more than one piece—even though we never did! . . . The meals were so generous that we usually did not eat an evening meal if we ate the noon meal at the restaurant.

—ESTHER SHANK, *MENNONITE COUNTRY-STYLE RECIPES AND KITCHEN SECRETS*

Virginia's Almost Impossible Coconut Pie

MAKES ONE 9-INCH PIE

"Impossible" pies, which were popular in the 1960s, are made with Bisquick instead of pie crust. This recipe, from Mildred's sister Virginia, isn't authentically "impossible" because it doesn't use Bisquick. Instead, the filling makes its own firmer layer of custard next to the pie plate as it bakes, forming a sort of crust. It's simply perfect for the crust-shy baker. The coconut on top of this pie is nice and crunchy, providing a delightful contrast to the creamy custard.

Preheat the oven to 350°F. Lightly grease a pie plate with butter or cooking spray.

Stir the eggs and milk together in a bowl, then stir in the sugar, flour, and coconut. Add the butter and vanilla and mix well.

Pour into a 9-inch pie plate and bake for about 35 to 40 minutes, until set and golden brown. The filling should wobble very slightly in the center when the pan is jiggled. Custards continue to cook when taken out of the oven, so don't overdo it. Cool on a wire rack for 1 hour before slicing. Serve at room temperature or chilled.

2 eggs, lightly beaten

1 cup whole milk

1 cup sugar

¼ cup self-rising flour

1⅓ cups sweetened flaked coconut

¼ cup unsalted butter, melted

1 teaspoon vanilla extract

Original Coconut Cream Pie

MAKES ONE 9-INCH PIE

This is the most popular dessert at Mrs. Rowe's Restaurant and Bakery. Enough said.

½ recipe Plain Pie Pastry (page 17)
   or Vinegar Pie Crust (page 19),
   prebaked

3 eggs yolks

1 cup sugar

¼ cup cornstarch

¼ to ½ cup water

3 cups whole milk

1 cup sweetened flaked coconut

1 tablespoon unsalted butter

2 teaspoons vanilla extract

1 recipe Mrs. Rowe's Meringue
   (page 24)

Preheat the oven to 325°F.

Stir together the egg yolks, sugar, cornstarch, and just enough of the water to make a smooth paste. Heat the milk in a double boiler set over simmering water. When the milk begins to steam, gradually whisk in the egg mixture. Cook, stirring occasionally, until very thick, about 4 minutes. Remove from the heat and stir in ¾ cup of the coconut, the butter, and the vanilla.

Pour the filling into the crust and top with the meringue, sealing the edges well. Sprinkle the remaining ¼ cup coconut over the meringue.

Bake for about 30 minutes, until the meringue is golden brown and it's firm to the careful touch (it's easy to poke a hole in the meringue). Cool on a wire rack for 2 hours before slicing. Serve the pie at room temperature or, for a special treat, serve it warm—pop a slice in the microwave for about 10 seconds.

Coconut Custard Pie

MAKES ONE 9-INCH PIE

This recipe was found in a notebook belonging to Willard Rowe (Mildred's second husband), on a stained and yellowed sheet of ruled paper. Willard died in 1972, but many of his recipes are still used by the family and the business. This pie is a favorite of longtime customers Marion and Gene Harner, who remember when Mrs. Rowe's Restaurant included a slice of pie with every meal. "You got a complete meal for under $2," says Gene.

½ recipe Plain Pie Pastry (page 17) or Vinegar Pie Crust (page 19)

3 cups whole milk

3 egg yolks

¾ cup sugar

¼ cup cornstarch

1 teaspoon water

1 tablespoon unsalted butter

1 teaspoon vanilla extract

½ cup coconut

Preheat the oven to 350°F. Line a 9-inch pie plate with the rolled-out crust.

Bring the milk to a boil in a large saucepan over medium heat. Separately, mix the egg yolks, sugar, cornstarch, and water to make a smooth paste. Gradually stir the yolk mixture into the milk and cook, whisking constantly, until it thickens, about 20 minutes. The mixture should coat a spoon, and a line drawn across the spoon will stay clear. Remove from the heat and stir in the butter and vanilla.

Sprinkle half of the coconut in the crust in an even layer, pour in the filling, then sprinkle the remaining coconut over the top.

Bake for 45 to 55 minutes, or until almost completely set. The filling should wobble very slightly in the center when the pan is jiggled. Custards continue to cook when taken out of the oven, so don't overdo it. Cool on a wire rack to room temperature for 1 hour, then chill for 1 hour. Serve cold.

White Christmas Pie

MAKES ONE 9-INCH PIE

This recipe was found in a notebook belonging to Bertha, one of Mildred's sisters. It was clipped out of an old newspaper and pasted onto a page of the notebook. It's a festive-looking and showy pie offering a delicate almond-coconut flavor and a spongy, frothy texture somewhere between meringue and marshmallow, with a hint of chewiness from the coconut. It makes a delightful addition to any holiday table.

Soften the gelatin in the cold water. Combine ½ cup of the sugar with the flour and salt in a saucepan. Gradually stir in the milk and cook over medium heat, stirring constantly, until mixture thickens and comes to a boil. Boil for 1 minute, stirring constantly. Remove from the heat and stir in the gelatin, vanilla extract, and almond extract. Cool until lukewarm.

Beat the egg whites and cream of tartar with an electric mixer on slow to medium speed until foamy, then add the remaining ¼ cup sugar, 1 tablespoon at a time, and continue beating until soft peaks form. Fold the egg whites, whipped cream, and coconut into the gelatin mixture, then pour into the crust. Sprinkle with additional coconut if you like.

Chill until set, about 3 to 4 hours, before slicing. Garnish with candied cherries if you like. Serve cold.

½ recipe Plain Pie Pastry (page 17) or Vinegar Pie Crust (page 19), prebaked

3 ounces unflavored gelatin

¼ cup cold water

¾ cup sugar

¼ cup all-purpose flour

½ teaspoon salt

1½ cups whole milk

¾ teaspoon vanilla extract

¼ teaspoon almond extract

3 egg whites, at room temperature

¼ teaspoon cream of tartar

½ cup heavy cream, whipped to medium peaks

1 cup sweetened flaked coconut, plus more for sprinkling (optional)

Red and green candied cherries, for garnish (optional)

Susan's Banana Cream Pie

MAKES ONE 9-INCH PIE

Here's another recipe from Susan Simmons, a longtime baker at Mrs. Rowe's Country Buffet who now works in the catering arm. Pouring the hot custard over the bananas infuses an incredible banana flavor into the creamy custard, making for an ultimate pie experience. When you prepare the egg yolks for the custard, remember to save the whites for the meringue!

½ recipe Plain Pie Pastry (page 17) or Vinegar Pie Crust (page 19), prebaked

3 egg yolks

1 cup sugar

¼ cup cornstarch

3 cups whole milk

1 tablespoon unsalted butter

2 teaspoons vanilla extract

1 medium banana, sliced

1 recipe Mrs. Rowe's Meringue (page 24)

Preheat the oven to 325°F.

Mix the egg yolks, sugar, and cornstarch together. Using a double boiler, heat the milk until it boils. Whisk in the egg mixture and cook, stirring occasionally with the whisk, for about 4 minutes, until very thick. Remove from the heat and stir in the butter and vanilla.

Slice the banana and arrange the slices in the crust. Pour the filling over the bananas and top with the meringue, sealing the edges well.

Bake for about 30 minutes, until golden brown. The filling should wobble very slightly in the center when the pan is jiggled. Custards continue to cook when taken out of the oven, so don't overdo it. Cool to room temperature on a wire rack, then chill in the refrigerator for 3 to 4 hours before slicing. Serve cold.

Classic Banana Cream Pie

MAKES ONE 9-INCH PIE

Roger Bible, a relative of the Rowe family, says "My favorite pie is Mildred's banana cream, which she often brought along to family gatherings. I think it was the best thing I've ever eaten in my life."

½ recipe Plain Pie Pastry (page 17)
    or Vinegar Pie Crust (page 19),
    prebaked

3 tablespoons cornstarch

1⅔ cups water

1 (14-ounce) can sweetened
    condensed milk

3 egg yolks, beaten

2 tablespoons unsalted butter

1 teaspoon vanilla extract

3 medium bananas

½ cup lemon juice, for dipping

Sweetened Whipped Cream (page 26),
    for topping

Whisk the cornstarch into the water in a heavy saucepan, then stir in the milk and egg yolks. Cook over medium heat, whisking constantly, for about 10 minutes, until thick and bubbly. The whisk should leave tracks in the thickened mixture. Remove from the heat, stir in the butter and vanilla, and let cool slightly.

Slice 2 of the bananas ⅛ to ¼ inch thick. Put half of the lemon juice in a small bowl and dip the bananas into it, gently tossing to evenly coat. Drain off any excess lemon juice and arrange the banana slices in the crust. Spread the filling evenly over the bananas and cover with plastic wrap directly on the cream (this prevents a skin from forming).

Chill for 4 hours, until set. Spread the whipped cream on top. Slice the remaining banana, dip it into the remaining lemon juice, and gently toss to evenly coat. Drain off any excess lemon juice and garnish the top of the pie with the banana slices.

Store in the refrigerator for at least 30 minutes, preferably 3 to 4 hours, before slicing. Serve cold.

Sour Cream and Raisin Pie

MAKES ONE 9-INCH PIE

Mrs. Rowe attributed this recipe to her friend Mrs. John Martin, a Mennonite from Harrisonburg. The custard is slightly grainy, which is normal for this old-fashioned pie, and its pleasant, refreshing flavor is unusual to the modern palate. For plumper raisins, bring them to a boil in a small amount of water, then lower the heat and simmer for 20 minutes. Drain the raisins thoroughly before proceeding with the recipe.

In a double boiler, stir the sugar, cornstarch, and salt together, then add the eggs, sour cream, lemon juice, and baking soda. Cook, stirring constantly, for about 35 minutes, until thick. Gently stir in the raisins.

Pour the filling into a shallow container, lay plastic wrap directly on the surface, and chill in the refrigerator for 30 minutes.

Pour the filling into the crust and sprinkle with the coconut. Chill for several hours or overnight before slicing. Serve cold.

½ recipe Plain Pie Pastry (page 17) or Vinegar Pie Crust (page 19), prebaked

¾ cup sugar

2 tablespoons cornstarch

¼ teaspoon salt

2 eggs, beaten

1½ cups sour cream

1 tablespoon lemon juice

½ teaspoon baking soda

1¼ cups raisins

⅛ cup sweetened flaked coconut, for sprinkling

Strawberry Sour Cream Pie

MAKES ONE 9-INCH PIE

This filling, which has a pleasant tartness, bakes up like a firm custard. The pie is at its best when served slightly warm. If it's been in the refrigerator, 20 seconds in the microwave is all it takes to warm up a slice for that just-baked sensation.

½ recipe Plain Pie Pastry (page 17) or Vinegar Pie Crust (page 19), parbaked

FILLING

2 eggs, at room temperature

2 cups sour cream, at room temperature

⅓ cup all-purpose flour

¼ cup sugar

½ teaspoon vanilla extract

½ teaspoon grated orange zest

Pinch of salt

1 pound fresh strawberries, sliced

STREUSEL TOPPING

3 tablespoons all-purpose flour

2 tablespoons brown sugar

1 tablespoon unsalted butter, melted

Preheat the oven to 350°F.

To make the filling, whisk the eggs until frothy. Add the sour cream, flour, sugar, vanilla, orange zest, and salt and whisk until completely blended.

Spread the strawberries in the crust in an even layer and pour the filling over them.

To make the topping, combine the flour, brown sugar, and butter in a small bowl and mix thoroughly. Sprinkle the streusel evenly over the filling.

Bake for 50 to 55 minutes, using pie shields or foil if the crust is overbrowning, until the top puffs up slightly and the filling is set but springy. The filling won't brown. Cool to room temperature on a wire rack, about 30 minutes, or serve slightly warm.

Never-Fail Lemon Pie

MAKES ONE 9-INCH PIE

This pie is unbelievably easy—you really can't fail. You could make this pie in a plain pie crust, but why would you want to when this sweet and spicy alternative is available? When you prepare the egg yolks for the filling, remember to save the whites for the meringue.

Preheat the oven to 325°F.

Combine the lemon juice and extract, then slowly pour in the milk and blend with an electric mixer on low speed. Add the egg yolks and continue mixing until well blended. Pour the lemon filling into the crust. Top off with the meringue.

Bake for about 15 to 20 minutes, until the meringue is lightly browned. Cool on a wire rack for 1 hour before slicing. Serve at room temperature or chilled.

1 recipe Gingersnap Crust (page 22), baked

½ cup lemon juice

¼ teaspoon lemon extract

1 (14-ounce) can sweetened condensed milk

2 egg yolks

1 recipe Mrs. Rowe's Meringue (page 24) or Weepless Meringue (page 25)

Key Lime (or Not) Pie

MAKES ONE 9-INCH PIE

If you don't like the texture of lime zest in an otherwise smooth and silky filling, feel free to leave it out. Although it isn't really a Key lime pie without Key lime juice, regular lime juice is just as delicious in this pie. For those who like a wonderfully tart pie, serve it plain, or you can top it with a dollop of whipped cream. If the pie sticks to the pan when you're scooping it out, try dipping the bottom of the pan into a bowl of warm water to loosen it.

Preheat the oven to 325°F.

Whisk the egg yolks and lime zest together in a bowl for about 2 minutes, until a light greenish yellow color. Whisk in the milk, then the lime juice, and set aside at room temperature for about 5 minutes, until the filling thickens and the whisk leaves tracks in it. Spread the filling evenly in the crust.

Bake for about 15 minutes, until almost completely set. The filling should wobble a bit when the pan is jiggled. Cool to room temperature on a wire rack, then chill in the refrigerator for at least 3 hours before slicing.

1 recipe Graham Cracker Crust (page 23), prebaked

4 egg yolks

1 rounded tablespoon grated lime zest

1 (14-ounce) can sweetened condensed milk

½ cup freshly squeezed lime juice, made with Key limes or regular limes

Chocolate Chess Pie

MAKES ONE 9-INCH PIE

This rich pie is creamy on the inside and crusty on the outside—a treat for those who love chocolate, as well as for those who love interesting contrasts in texture. Serve cold for the best flavor.

½ recipe Plain Pie Pastry (page 17)
　　or Vinegar Pie Crust (page 19)

1½ cups sugar

3½ tablespoons cocoa

Pinch of salt

1 (12-ounce) can evaporated milk

2 eggs, beaten

¼ cup unsalted butter, melted

1 teaspoon vanilla extract

Preheat the oven to 350°F. Line a 9-inch pie plate with the rolled-out crust.

Mix the sugar, cocoa, and salt together, then blend in the milk, eggs, butter, and vanilla. Pour the filling into the crust.

Bake for 45 to 50 minutes, until almost completely set. The filling should wobble very slightly in the center when the pan is jiggled. Cool to room temperature on a wire rack, then chill in the refrigerator for 2 to 3 hours or overnight before slicing. Serve chilled.

Pie, we'd found, often acted as a wooden spoon, stirring up the soul.

—PASCALE LE DRAOULEC, *AMERICAN PIE: SLICES OF LIFE (AND PIE) FROM AMERICA'S BACK ROADS*

Tar Heel Pie

MAKES ONE 9-INCH PIE

This luscious pie recipe was found handwritten in Mildred's notebook. She might have gotten it from relatives in North Carolina. Once it's completely cool, the pie sets up firm and can be sliced neatly, but it's also delicious as a warm, gooey mess. Chef William Poole, of Wen Chocolates in Denver, Colorado, says, "This is the best pie I've ever had, except for my grandmother's pumpkin pie." It's wonderful served topped with ice cream or whipped cream.

Preheat the oven to 350°F. Line a 9-inch pie plate with the rolled-out crust.

Put the chocolate chips in a bowl, pour in the melted butter, and stir until the chocolate is mostly melted. Add the pecans, flour, sugars, eggs, vanilla, and salt, and stir until thoroughly combined. Pour the filling into the crust.

Bake for 30 to 40 minutes, until the filling forms a smooth brown crust and begins to pull away from the pie crust. Custards continue to cook when taken out of the oven, so don't overdo it. The filling will still be wet in the center but will firm up as it cools.

Cool on a wire rack for about 1 hour before slicing. Serve at room temperature or slightly warm.

½ recipe Plain Pie Pastry (page 17)
  or Vinegar Pie Crust (page 19)

1 cup semisweet or dark chocolate chips

½ cup unsalted butter, melted

1 cup pecans

½ cup all-purpose flour

½ cup sugar

½ cup brown sugar

2 eggs

1 teaspoon vanilla extract

Pinch of salt

German Chocolate Pie

MAKES ONE 9-INCH PIE

Mrs. Rowe's restaurants serve this luscious dream of a pie for chocolate lovers only on special occasions—but you can make it anytime at home.

To make the filling, combine the sugar and cornstarch in a saucepan, then stir in the milk, chocolate, and butter. Cook over medium-high heat, whisking constantly, until thickened and bubbly. Turn down the heat to medium and continue to cook and whisk another 2 minutes. Gradually stir about 1 cup of the hot mixture into the egg yolks, then pour the yolk mixture into the saucepan. Return to a boil over medium heat and cook and whisk another 2 minutes. Remove from heat and stir in the vanilla, then pour the filling into the crust.

To make the topping, combine the egg, milk, sugar, and butter in a saucepan over medium heat. Cook and stir until just thickened and bubbly. Remove from the heat and stir in the coconut and pecans, then spread the topping evenly over the chocolate filling.

Cool to room temperature on a wire rack, then chill in the refrigerator for several hours before slicing. Serve chilled.

½ recipe Plain Pie Pastry (page 17) or Vinegar Pie Crust (page 19), prebaked

FILLING

⅓ cup sugar

3 tablespoons cornstarch

1½ cups whole milk

4 ounces German sweet cooking chocolate, chopped

1 tablespoon unsalted butter

2 egg yolks, beaten

1 teaspoon vanilla extract

TOPPING

1 egg, beaten

1 (5-ounce) can evaporated milk

½ cup sugar

¼ cup unsalted butter

1⅓ cups sweetened flaked coconut

½ cup chopped pecans

Willard's Chocolate Pie

MAKES ONE 9-INCH PIE

This recipe was found in a little brown book that belonged to Willard, Mrs. Rowe's second husband. This pie is time-consuming to make, but well worth the effort for those who love milk chocolate. It's as smooth as a creamy chocolate popsicle. Try it with the Gingersnap Crust (page 22) for a flavorful interplay between smooth and spicy. Serve chilled.

½ recipe Plain Pie Pastry (page 17) or Vinegar Pie Crust (page 19), prebaked

3 cups whole milk

3 egg yolks

¾ cup sugar

¼ cup cocoa

¼ cup cornstarch

¼ to ½ cup water

1 tablespoon unsalted butter

1 teaspoon vanilla extract

Bring the milk to a simmer in a large saucepan over medium heat. Vigilance is required so that the milk does not burn. In the top of a double boiler (off the heat), mix the egg yolks, sugar, cocoa, cornstarch, and just enough of the water to make a smooth paste. Use as little water as possible; it's okay for the paste to be thick. Slowly pour the milk into the egg yolk mixture while whisking continuously, then place over simmering water in the bottom of the double boiler and cook, stirring frequently, for 45 minutes, until quite thick with a puddinglike consistency. Remove from the heat and stir in the butter and vanilla.

Pour the filling into a shallow container, lay plastic wrap directly on the surface, and chill in the refrigerator for about 1 hour, until cold.

Scrape the filling into the crust and refrigerate about 3 to 5 hours, until set. Serve cold.

Chocolate Meringue Pie

MAKES ONE 9-INCH PIE

This pie, one of the most popular at the Staunton eatery, has a medium-dark chocolate filling topped off with mounds of fresh meringue. Vivian Obie, a cook and baker for the restaurant for over forty years, remembers her first day as a baker, which was an Easter Sunday—one of the busiest days of the year. She recalls using this recipe to make chocolate pie: "The baker who usually made the chocolate pie called in sick. I thought I could do it. I made it and it looked so pretty with the meringue on it and all. I thought I had it made. But when they sliced it, the pie ran all over the place. The chocolate just wasn't thick enough." If you follow the instructions and make sure the pie is cooled completely, then don't worry—it will turn out great.

Preheat the oven to 325°F.

Stir together the egg yolks, sugar, cocoa, cornstarch, and just enough of the water to make a smooth paste. Heat the milk in a double boiler set over simmering water. When the milk begins to steam, gradually whisk in the egg mixture. Cook, stirring occasionally, until very thick, about 4 minutes. Remove from the heat and stir in the butter and vanilla, then pour the filling into the crust. Top with the meringue, sealing the edges well.

Bake for about 30 minutes, until the meringue is golden brown. Cool for at least 1 hour on a wire rack before slicing. Serve at room temperature or chilled.

½ recipe Plain Pie Pastry (page 17) or Vinegar Pie Crust (page 19), prebaked

3 egg yolks

1 cup sugar

¼ cup cocoa

¼ cup cornstarch

½ to ¾ cup water

3 cups whole milk

1 tablespoon unsalted butter

2 teaspoons vanilla extract

1 recipe Mrs. Rowe's Meringue (page 24)

Smoothest Ever Peanut Butter Pie

MAKES ONE 9-INCH PIE

The texture of this pie is creamier and smoother than the version that Mrs. Rowe's restaurants serve, which was included in Mrs. Rowe's Restaurant Cookbook: A Lifetime of Recipes from the Shenandoah Valley. *For smooth peanut butter fans, this pie is hard to beat. The recipe comes from Susan Simmons, a baker for Mrs. Rowe's Catering.*

½ recipe Plain Pie Pastry (page 17) or Vinegar Pie Crust (page 19), prebaked

⅓ cup creamy peanut butter

¾ cup confectioners' sugar

FILLING

½ cup sugar

⅓ cup all-purpose flour

⅛ teaspoon salt

2 cups whole milk

2 egg yolks, slightly beaten

2 teaspoons unsalted butter

1 teaspoon vanilla extract

Whipped topping or Sweetened Whipped Cream (page 26), for topping

Combine the peanut butter and confectioners' sugar and mix with a fork until crumbly. Reserve 2 tablespoons of the mixture and sprinkle the rest in the crust.

To make the filling, put the sugar, flour, and salt in a saucepan and stir to combine. Add the milk and egg yolks, then place over medium heat. Cook and stir for about 10 minutes, until bubbly and thickened. Remove from the heat and stir in the butter and vanilla.

Pour the filling into the crust, then chill in the refrigerator for 1 hour, until set.

Spread the whipped topping over the pie and sprinkle with the reserved peanut butter mixture before serving. Served chilled.

Peanut Butter Custard Pie

Peanuts are grown in the southeastern part of Virginia but enjoyed throughout the state, especially in pie. The crunchy peanut butter crumbles and the smoothness of the custard pair for a scrumptious pie experience. For an interesting take on the classic combination of chocolate and peanut butter, try it in the Chocolate Cookie Crust (page 21). If you have trouble finding custard mix at the store, you can either look for it online or substitute the custard part of a package of instant flan mix.

Combine the peanut butter and confectioners' sugar and mix with a fork until crumbly. Reserve ¼ cup of the mixture and sprinkle the rest in the crust.

Prepare the custard with the milk according to the package instructions. Pour the prepared custard filling into the crust, then chill for about 30 minutes, until set.

Spread the whipped cream over the pie and sprinkle with the reserved peanut butter mixture before serving. Serve chilled.

½ recipe Plain Pie Pastry (page 17) or Vinegar Pie Crust (page 19), prebaked

½ cup chunky peanut butter

1 cup confectioners' sugar

1 (3-ounce) package custard mix

2 cups whole milk

Sweetened Whipped Cream, without the vanilla (page 26), for topping

Cinnamon Sugar Pie

MAKES ONE 9-INCH PIE

Velvety smooth, fragrant, and creamy, this is a warming and perfectly soothing pie.

½ recipe Plain Pie Pastry (page 17) or Vinegar Pie Crust (page 19), prebaked

3 eggs, beaten

¼ cup unsalted butter

1 cup sugar

3 tablespoons cornstarch

1 teaspoon ground cinnamon

1 teaspoon ground allspice

½ teaspoon ground cloves

2 cups half-and-half

1 teaspoon vanilla extract

1 recipe Weepless Meringue (page 25)

Combine the eggs, butter, sugar, cornstarch, cinnamon, allspice, and cloves in a saucepan and stir until thoroughly combined. Slowly pour in the half-and-half, stirring constantly. Cook over low heat, stirring constantly, for about 25 minutes, until thick and smooth. Remove from the heat and stir in the vanilla.

Pour the filling into a shallow container, lay plastic wrap directly on the surface, and chill in the refrigerator for about 2 hours, until cold.

Scrape the filling into the crust and return to the refrigerator for 2 to 3 hours.

Preheat the oven to 325°F.

Top the pie with the meringue, sealing the edges well.

Bake for 20 minutes, just until the meringue is lightly browned. Cool to room temperature on a wire rack before slicing. Serve at room temperature or chilled.

CHAPTER 4

Frozen and Icebox Pies

I have researched pie all over the country and in Canada, and I can tell you that people in the South have a deep long-standing relationship with pie. It's not just a crush, it's true love.

—STEPHANIE ANDERSON WITMER, AUTHOR OF *KILLER PIES*

COOL TREATS FOR HOT SOUTHERN DAYS

The patchwork of geographic diversity of the South—from the bayous and swamps to the mountains and oceans—has one binding trait: summer is hot, so eating lighter and keeping cool is an annual pastime. Summer food is an important part of the ritual, even in today's air-conditioned South, where the days of sipping mint juleps under the magnolia tree are long gone—well, for the most part.

A cool, no-bake pie is a manageable temptation on long, hot days. With just the right puff of texture and flavor, a slice of icebox pie is still a light and tasty way to end the day. No-bake recipes were popular during the Great Depression, when Mildred Rowe came of age. Perhaps that's why she delighted in these pies. Even as technology progressed and America became electrified, large chunks of rural America still didn't have electricity, let alone refrigerators, so food was often kept cool in a root cellar, springhouse, or icebox—the latter lending its name to these cool pies. But keeping frozen treats like ice cream cold enough was impossible except in wintertime, or if the family had an icehouse, which was an expensive structure. And, of course, freezing temperatures in the wintertime aren't a given in much of the South, as they are in Virginia's Appalachia, with its cold and snowy winters.

Mike DiGrassie remembers eating a cold treat in the middle of winter: snow "ice cream." He didn't know he was participating in an old custom, probably stretching back to ancient China, of using natural ice and snow to make cold refreshments and keep them cold. "We gathered the snow and mixed it with vanilla and sugar, and sometimes a little milk. It was so good and so simple," Mike says.

Not so simple, however, is the delectable treat of ice cream pie. At one time it was considered chic, since only those with freezers and time on their hands could make it. Even today, with all of our modern conveniences, our recipe tester, Kate Antea, says that the ice cream pie recipe "is an exercise in time management." But for ice cream lovers it's an effort worth making, just for that refreshing explosion of flavors and textures, setting tongues to quiver.

This section offers pies at both ends of the time spectrum, from easily whipped-up concoctions like the Make-Your-Own-Flavor Chiffon Pie (page 99) to the Layered Ice Cream Pie (page 96). But all have one thing in common—they're a delicious way to cool off on hot summer days.

Most of these pies are too delicate to withstand the hectic rigors of the restaurants. They're fragile and not easy to keep on hand, so they aren't served at

Mrs. Rowe's restaurants on a daily basis, though they are sometimes offered on special occasions like Mother's Day, Father's Day, and various holidays. But summer in the South begs for light, cold, and sweet refreshments, and Mrs. Rowe and her family often indulged in cold or icy pie, so we've included a selection of favorites in this cookbook.

Pie's Safe!

In the 1960s and 1970s, before the days of complicated alarm systems, Mrs. Rowe developed a reliable antitheft system with her pie. All the local police officers and state troopers who worked the night shift knew there was a free slice of pie waiting for them at break time—close to closing time at the restaurant. It worked out well. There was always a police presence at closing time, which made her feel safe, and it appealed to Mrs. Rowe's sense of thriftiness—it proved to be a great way to make use of leftover pie at the end of the evening.

Frozen Strawberry Daiquiri Pie

MAKES ONE 9-INCH PIE

Smooth, firm, and creamy, this pie is naturally a lovely shade of pink, so you need not add the food coloring unless you want a deeper color. After 6 hours in the freezer, it's slice-able but still soft. Left overnight, it's firm but still creamy—a little piece of strawberry heaven.

Beat the cream cheese with an electric mixer on medium speed until fluffy. Gradually pour in the milk and continue beating until smooth. Stir in the daiquiri mix and rum, and the food coloring if you like. Fold in the whipped topping.

Pour the filling into the crust and freeze for at least 6 hours, or preferably overnight.

1 recipe Graham Cracker Crust (page 23), baked

1 (8-ounce) package cream cheese, at room temperature

1 (14-ounce) can sweetened condensed milk

⅔ cup frozen strawberry daiquiri mix, thawed

2 tablespoons light rum

1 to 2 drops red food coloring (optional)

1 cup whipped topping, thawed according to package directions

Frozen Strawberry Margarita Pie

MAKES ONE 9-INCH PIE

The icy strawberry filling in this pie is pleasantly complemented by the luscious whipped cream. The pie tastes just like a margarita—the tequila flavor adds quite a zing. The recipe calls for freezing the whipped cream on top of the pie, but you can also freeze just the strawberry part and add the whipped cream when you serve the pie.

1 recipe Chocolate Cookie Crust (page 21), baked and chilled

1 (20-ounce) package frozen strawberries, thawed and drained

¾ cup plus 2 tablespoons sugar

¼ cup tequila

1 tablespoon lime juice

2 cups heavy cream

In food processor or blender, puree the strawberries with the ¾ cup sugar, the tequila, and the lime juice. Transfer to a bowl.

Beat ½ cup of the cream with an electric mixer at high speed until stiff peaks form. Using a wire whisk, fold the whipped cream into the strawberry mixture. Pour half the strawberry mixture into the crust. Cover the pie and the remaining filling with plastic wrap and freeze for 2 hours.

Remove the plastic wrap and spread the remaining filling over the frozen pie, mounding it slightly in the center. Freeze for about 2 hours or overnight, until firm.

Combine the remaining 1½ cups cream and the 2 tablespoons sugar and beat with an electric mixer on medium-high to high speed until stiff peaks form. Spread the whipped cream over the frozen pie and return it to the freezer until ready to serve.

Watermelon Pie

MAKES ONE 9-INCH PIE

Fresh watermelon is a summertime treat throughout the South, where the melons can be seen sprawled in many backyard gardens. These days, watermelon can be bought almost any time of year at most grocery stores. This pretty pink pie makes a spectacular offering at a special brunch.

Dissolve the gelatin in the boiling water in a small bowl. Let cool to room temperature, then whisk in the whipped topping until completely blended. Drain off any watermelon liquid that has seeped out, then fold the watermelon cubes into the filling.

Spoon the filling into the crust and chill for 2 to 3 hours or overnight before slicing.

1 recipe Graham Cracker Crust (page 23), baked

1 (3-ounce) package watermelon gelatin

¼ cup boiling water

12 ounces whipped topping, thawed according to package directions

2 cups cubed seedless watermelon

According to *Sook's Cookbook: Memories and Traditional Receipts from the Deep South*, by Marie Rudisill, there is an old superstition in the South that one should save the pointed tip of a slice of pie for the last bite.

Peanut Pie

MAKES ONE 9-INCH PIE

Stephen Harriman, a writer for the Norfolk Virginian-Pilot, *says, "For some reason, I was expecting the peanut pie to be a pecan pie look-alike. Instead it looked more like a lemon meringue or banana cream pie. If you like peanuts smooth, you'll love this."*

1 recipe Graham Cracker Crust (page 23), baked

4 ounces cream cheese, at room temperature

1 cup confectioners' sugar

½ cup creamy peanut butter

½ cup whole milk

9 ounces whipped topping or 2⅓ cups Sweetened Whipped Cream (page 26)

¼ cup finely chopped salted peanuts

Beat the cream cheese with an electric mixer on medium speed until soft and fluffy. Add the sugar and peanut butter and continue mixing, then slowly pour in the milk and mix until thoroughly combined. Spread the filling evenly in the crust, top with the whipped topping, and sprinkle with the peanuts.

Freeze for at least 1 hour, until firm, before slicing. Don't try to wrap the pie in plastic wrap until it's frozen firm.

When I moved here about thirteen years ago, all I heard is that I needed to go to Mrs. Rowe's to try the pie. I thought people were crazy—restaurant pie is never good. But it turned out the pie was good and reminded me of my mother's homemade pie.

—EILEEN REED, CUSTOMER

Mudd Pie

MAKES ONE DEEP-DISH 10-INCH PIE

Mudd Pie is a rich treat that's fun to make; you simply can't go wrong with it! It's a fun kitchen activity for children, too, and they love to eat the results.

Set the ice cream out to soften.

Combine the chocolate chips, marshmallows, and milk in a small saucepan. When the milk begins to steam, start stirring and continue until the chips and marshmallows are completely melted and the mixture is smooth. Let cool.

Spoon half of the ice cream into the crust, cover with half of the chocolate mixture, then repeat the layers. Top with the walnuts. Freeze for at least 30 minutes before serving.

1 recipe Chocolate Cookie Crust (page 21), baked in a deep 10-inch pie plate and chilled

1 cup semisweet chocolate chips

⅔ cup marshmallows

1 (5-ounce) can evaporated milk

1 quart coffee ice cream

½ cup chopped walnuts

Grasshopper Pie

MAKES ONE 9-INCH PIE

According to Retro Desserts, *by Wayne Brachman, this recipe dates back to the 1950s and was developed by a company that makes crème de menthe. Other recipes use a filling more like a Key lime pie, but made with mint. This version is mildly minty and has a texture like frozen cream. It's a pretty, delicate shade of green even without the food coloring.*

1 recipe Chocolate Cookie Crust (page 21), baked and chilled

¾ cup whole milk

24 large marshmallows (just over 6 ounces)

¼ cup crème de menthe

2 tablespoons white crème de cacao

1 to 2 drops green food coloring (optional)

1 cup heavy cream, whipped to firm peaks

Heat the milk in a saucepan over medium heat until warm, then add the marshmallows and continue to cook and stir until the marshmallows are melted and the mixture is smooth. Cool until lukewarm.

Add the liqueurs and mix well, then stir in a drop or two of green food coloring if you like. Fold in the whipped cream.

Spread the filling in the crust and freeze for 3 or 4 hours, until firm, before slicing.

Layered Ice Cream Pie

MAKES ONE 10-INCH PIE

This recipe appeared in the restaurant's self-published cookbook, which notes that you should "serve only to those who truly appreciate dessert and won't complain about calories." This pie reminds me of a quote from Chocolat, *the movie based on the book by Joanne Harris: "It melts ever so slightly on your tongue and tortures you with pleasure."*

1¼ cups crushed plain chocolate cookies (without icing or filling)

3 tablespoons unsalted butter, melted

¾ to 1 cup Caramel Sauce (page 27)

1 quart chocolate ice cream, softened

1 quart vanilla ice cream, softened

6 (1.4-ounce) Heath bars or toffee-flavored candy bars, crushed

¾ to 1 cup Chocolate Sauce (page 28)

1 quart coffee ice cream, softened

Preheat the oven to 350°F.

Combine the cookie crumbs and butter and mix well. Firmly and evenly press the mixture over the bottom of a 3-inch-deep 10-inch springform pan. Bake for 8 minutes, then cool on a wire rack for at least 30 minutes, until it's no longer warm to the touch.

Spread the caramel sauce over the cooled crust, leaving a 1-inch border. Freeze for about 30 to 60 minutes, until set.

Spread the chocolate ice cream over the caramel sauce in an even layer, then freeze for about for 30 to 60 minutes, until firm. (Freezing time depends on the quality of the ice cream and the freezer temperature.)

Combine the vanilla ice cream and crushed candy bars. Spread over the chocolate ice cream in an even layer, then freeze for about 30 minutes, until firm.

Spread a thin layer of chocolate sauce evenly over the vanilla ice cream, then freeze for about 30 minutes, until firm.

Spread the coffee ice cream over the chocolate sauce in an even layer, then return to the freezer for about 30 to 60 minutes, until firm. Cover tightly with plastic wrap and freeze for at least 8 hours before slicing.

Remove from the freezer about 10 minutes before serving. Remove the springform pan sides, and slice into 12 wedges. If you like, serve additional caramel and chocolate sauce on the side.

Time Management Advice from Pie Tester Kate Antea

This pie will take about 4 hours to make. While one layer is freezing, the next ice cream is out softening, and a sauce can be made and cooled. My suggestion is to start by making the caramel sauce (which can be done a day ahead). While the sauce cools, make the crust. While the caramel is freezing, take the chocolate ice cream out to soften. When the chocolate layer goes in to freeze, take out the vanilla ice cream to soften and chop the candy bars. When the vanilla layer goes in to freeze, make and cool the chocolate sauce. When the chocolate sauce layer goes in to freeze, take out the coffee ice cream to soften.

Caramel Coconut Pie

MAKES ONE 9-INCH DEEP-DISH PIE OR ONE 10-INCH REGULAR PIE

This recipe was in Mrs. Rowe's self-published cookbook, Mrs. Rowe's Favorite Recipes, which is no longer in print. A note at the bottom of the page gives low-fat options, like using low-fat cream cheese and margarine. Give it a whirl if you like, but you'd be missing out on the true-blue flavor of this pie. The coconut and pecans will need close attention while toasting; don't let their heavenly smell distract you. In fact, they continue to cook for a minute or so after being removed from the heat, so stop cooking them just before they look the way you want them to—golden brown and crunchy. Try the Chocolate Cookie Crust (page 21) for contrast, or the Gingersnap Crust (page 22) to cut the sweetness.

½ recipe Plain Pie Pastry (page 17) or Vinegar Pie Crust (page 19), prebaked

3 tablespoons unsalted butter

1⅓ cups sweetened flaked coconut

½ cup chopped pecans

4 ounces cream cheese, at room temperature

½ cup sweetened condensed milk

8 ounces whipped topping, thawed according to package directions

¾ cup Caramel Sauce (page 27) or store-bought caramel topping

Melt the butter in a heavy skillet over medium heat. Add the coconut and pecans and cook, stirring gently and frequently, until lightly browned.

Combine the cream cheese and milk and beat with an electric mixer on medium speed until smooth. Gently fold in the whipped topping, then pour half of the mixture into the crust. Warm the caramel in the microwave for 30 seconds and stir; this will make drizzling easier. Drizzle half of the caramel over the filling, and then sprinkle with about half of the coconut-pecan mixture. Repeat with another layer of filling, then caramel sauce, then coconut and pecans.

Cover the pie with plastic wrap and freeze for at least 8 hours. Let the pie stand at room temperature for 5 minutes before slicing.

Make-Your-Own-Flavor Chiffon Pie

MAKES TWO 9-INCH PIES

This pie offers a classic smooth texture and can feature any flavor you like. Here are a few suggestions: Try orange gelatin with pineapple juice, grape gelatin with grape juice, or raspberry gelatin with raspberry juice. It's a perfect light summer dessert, especially with complementary fresh fruit on the side.

Heat 1 cup of the juice and gelatin and stir until dissolved. Add the milk, whipped topping, lemon juice, and the remaining 1 cup fruit juice and whisk until thoroughly combined.

Divide the filling evenly between the 2 crusts, then refrigerate overnight before slicing.

2 recipes Graham Cracker Crust (page 23), baked

2 cups fruit juice

1 (3-ounce) package flavored gelatin

1 (14-ounce) can sweetened condensed milk

12 ounces whipped topping, thawed according to package directions

3 tablespoons lemon juice

CHAPTER 5

Pies for the Cupboard

The secret to the recipes is making them with a lot of love.

—LAURA ESQUIVEL, *LIKE WATER FOR CHOCOLATE*

LET THEM EAT PIE

Golden brown steaming pies on a farmhouse windowsill overlooking pastures with rolling mountains in the distance is a familiar sight in parts of the Shenandoah Valley. Some home kitchens and dining rooms also have one of the few pieces of furniture named and created for a food—the pie cupboard, also known as a pie chest or pie safe. Such is the esteem Americans hold for pie that we created a piece of furniture just to keep pies safe as they cool, away from children's probing fingers and other creatures' appetites.

Traditional pie chests have shallow shelves for pies and doors that close tightly. The doors often include tin panels with artful displays of holes punched in them, allowing the pies to breath. According to David Puckett and Karen Becker, staff at the Frontier Culture Museum in Staunton, Virginia, the first pie safes didn't have tin panels. Instead, cheesecloth or coarse linen was stretched across the cupboard doors.

Because sugar acts as a preservative, many pies actually don't need to be refrigerated and can be kept at room temperature for two to three days in a pie safe or on a kitchen counter—at home, that is. The standards for restaurants are, of course, different. Mike DiGrassie notes that most of his customers prefer pie at room temperature or slightly warm. "Years ago we kept our pies at room temperature all day. The Health Department changed their regulation on that. So now we keep them refrigerated and ask customers if they want their slice warmed."

The pies in this section aren't cream-based, fruit-filled, or chilled, so they don't fit into any of the other categories in this cookbook. Interestingly, some of these pies, like the shoofly, raisin, and chess pies, which come straight from the annals of history and are still being crafted today, weren't traditionally refrigerated. But as Esther Shank, author of *Mennonite Country-Style Recipes and Kitchen Secrets*, points out, pie storage is and was usually not much of an issue. Mike DiGrassie agrees. Whether it's served at home or in a restaurant, pie is one of the South's most time-honored, well-loved desserts, and it's usually eaten within a day of its baking.

Brown Sugar Pie

MAKES ONE 10-INCH PIE

This pie is as sweet and sticky as a pecan pie. Serve it with a scoop of vanilla ice cream, or cut the sweetness with a dollop of sour cream or unsweetened whipped cream.

½ recipe Plain Pie Pastry (page 17)
   or Vinegar Pie Crust (page 19)

1 cup white sugar

1 cup brown sugar

2 teaspoons all-purpose flour

3 eggs

½ cup unsalted butter, melted

2 teaspoons vanilla extract

Preheat the oven to 350°F. Line a 10-inch pie plate with the rolled-out crust.

Combine the sugars, flour, eggs, butter, and vanilla and beat for 3 minutes, using medium speed for a stand mixer, or high speed for a handheld mixer. Spread the filling evenly in the crust.

Bake for 50 to 60 minutes, until the filling forms a crisp, dark crust. Watch the pie during the last 10 minutes; if it starts to puff up, take it out of the oven. Cool on a wire rack for 1 to 2 hours before slicing.

Brown Sugar Pie from the Attic

MAKES ONE 9-INCH PIE

Mrs. Rowe's family is still finding recipe treasures scattered throughout her boxes and notes. Aaron found this recipe on an index card buried in a box in the attic. It's a sweet pie that tastes a lot like cookie dough.

Preheat the oven to 350°F. Line a 9-inch pie plate with the rolled-out crust. For a crispier crust, consider parbaking.

Cream the brown sugar and butter with an electric mixer at low speed until mixed thoroughly. Add the flour, salt, milk, eggs, and vanilla to the mixture and continue to blend until smooth and mixed thoroughly. Spread the filling evenly in the crust.

Bake for about 45 minutes, until the pie is a deep brown and a toothpick inserted near the center comes out clean. Cool on a wire rack for about 2 hours before slicing. Serve at room temperature.

½ recipe Plain Pie Pastry (page 17) or Vinegar Pie Crust, (page 19)

1 cup brown sugar

½ cup unsalted butter

3 tablespoons all-purpose flour

Pinch of salt

¼ cup sweetened condensed milk

2 eggs

1 teaspoon vanilla extract

Shoofly Pie

MAKES ONE 9-INCH PIE

In her book The Best of Amish Cooking, *Phyllis Pellman Good writes that shoofly pies may have been common in the past because "this hybrid cake within a pie shell" fared better than more delicate pies in the old-style bake ovens. With the advent of modern ovens, temperatures could be controlled, allowing for the development of the lighter pies that are standard today. Shoofly pies keep nicely in a pie cupboard. They also freeze well. This recipe uses ½ cup each of molasses and corn syrup for a sweeter flavor; you can simply use just a full cup of molasses, leaving out the corn syrup, for a stronger flavor if you like. This version also makes for a pie with a very wet bottom—the bottom of the crust disappears into the filling. If you'd like it drier, cut the water in the filling back to ¾ cup.*

Preheat the oven to 325°F. Line a 9-inch pie plate with the rolled-out crust.

To make the crumb topping, combine the flour, sugar, cinnamon, nutmeg, and butter and mix with a pastry blender or food processor until thoroughly combined and the mixture resembles fine crumbs.

To make the liquid bottom layer, mix the molasses and corn syrup, pour in the boiling water, and stir until evenly combined. Add the egg and baking soda and mix well.

Pour the liquid bottom layer into the crust, then sprinkle the crumb mixture over the top.

(continued)

½ recipe Plain Pie Pastry (page 17)
  or Vinegar Pie Crust (page 19)

CRUMB TOPPING

1 cup all-purpose flour

½ cup light brown sugar

1 teaspoon ground cinnamon

½ teaspoon ground nutmeg

⅓ cup cold unsalted butter

LIQUID BOTTOM

½ cup light molasses

½ cup dark corn syrup

1 cup boiling water

1 egg, beaten

1 teaspoon baking soda

Sweetened Whipped Cream (page 26),
for topping (optional)

Chocolate Sauce (page 28), for
drizzling (optional)

Bake for about 40 minutes, until medium set and dark brown. The filling should wobble very slightly in the center when the pan is jiggled, but a knife inserted in the center should come out clean. Cool on a wire rack for 1 to 2 hours before slicing. Serve warm or chilled, topped with a dollop of whipped cream or a drizzle of chocolate sauce if you like.

I understand the shoofly pie received its name because it attracted flies with its sweet syrupy base oozing slightly from the crumb topping, so youngsters were often called upon to stand by the shelf of pies to shoo the flies away since they were not refrigerated.

—ESTHER SHANK, *MENNONITE COUNTRY-STYLE RECIPES AND KITCHEN SECRETS*

Brownie Pie

MAKES ONE 9-INCH PIE

Aaron DiGrassie (Mrs. Rowe's grandson) picked up this fabulous, offbeat recipe when he worked at Ford's Colony in Williamsburg, Virginia. Now a new father and the restaurant's general manager, Aaron has come a long way since the day when he first started working in his grandmother's restaurant business. At the age of ten, the ambitious boy made and sold pie boxes for 10 cents each.

Preheat the oven to 375°F. Line a 9-inch pie plate with the rolled-out crust. For a crispier crust, consider parbaking.

Melt the chocolate and butter in a double boiler. Separately, cream the eggs and sugar with an electric mixer on medium speed until light in color. Add the corn syrup and the melted chocolate mixture and continue mixing until thoroughly combined. Spread the pecans in the crust in an even layer, then pour the filling over them.

Bake for 45 minutes for a really gooey center or 55 to 60 minutes for a firmer filling. At 45 minutes, a toothpick inserted 1 inch from the edge will come out clean, but the center will still wobble a bit when the pan is jiggled. At 55 minutes, the center will be set. The filling will puff up as it bakes and will deflate as it cools. Cool on a wire rack for at least 1 hour before slicing. Serve slightly warm or at room temperature.

½ recipe Plain Pie Pastry (page 17) or Vinegar Pie Crust (page 19)

2 ounces bittersweet chocolate

2 tablespoons unsalted butter

3 eggs

½ cup sugar

¾ cup dark corn syrup

1 cup chopped pecans

Pecan Fudge Pie

MAKES ONE 10-INCH PIE

Two sweet Southern favorites—pecans and fudge—come together in this extra-rich pie that bakes up like a big, soft brownie. Serve small slices topped with a dollop of unsweetened whipped cream, crème fraîche, or sour cream.

½ recipe Plain Pie Pastry (page 17)
   or Vinegar Pie Crust (page 19)

2 cups semisweet chocolate chips

4 eggs, beaten

1 cup light corn syrup

2 tablespoons unsalted butter, melted

2 teaspoons vanilla extract

½ teaspoon salt

1½ cups coarsely chopped pecans

Preheat the oven to 350°F. Line a 10-inch pie plate with the rolled-out crust.

Melt the chocolate chips in a double broiler, stirring occasionally. Combine the eggs, corn syrup, butter, vanilla, and salt and stir until thoroughly combined. Gradually add the chocolate to the egg mixture while stirring rapidly. Stir in the pecans. Spread the filling evenly in the crust.

Bake for 55 minutes, or until set, when a knife inserted in the center comes out clean. Cool on a wire rack for 1 hour before slicing. Serve at room temperature.

Raisin Pie

Amish and old-order Mennonites bake this pie, also called rosina *pie (German for rai-sin) or "funeral" pie, during any season. Some recipes include milk, making it more like a custard pie, and others use water, but they all seem to agree on the necessity of a double-crusted pie, often with a lattice top. If you like raisins, you'll love this pie. Walnuts, pecans, hazelnuts, or almonds would be perfect choices for the chopped nuts.*

Combine the raisins, water, and lemon juice in a heavy saucepan over medium-high heat and boil for about 20 minutes, until the raisins are plump. Drain the raisins and return them to the saucepan.

Combine the corn syrup, flour, and sugar, mix well, then add to the raisins and cook over medium-low heat for about 25 minutes, until thick. Look for a stiff consistency similar to mincemeat, with a thick, caramel-like sauce. Remove from the heat and stir in the nuts. Let cool.

Preheat the oven to 350°F. Line a 9-inch pie plate with 1 rolled-out crust. Spread the filling evenly in the crust. Brush the rim of the crust with the egg wash or water, cover with the second rolled-out crust, seal and flute or crimp the edges, and cut a few steam vents in the top. Brush the top with egg wash if you like.

Bake for 30 minutes, until golden brown. Cool on a wire rack for about 2 hours before slicing.

1 recipe Plain Pie Pastry (page 17) or Vinegar Pie Crust (page 19)

2½ cups raisins

1½ cups water

1 tablespoon lemon juice

¾ cup light corn syrup

2 tablespoons all-purpose flour

2 tablespoons sugar

½ cup coarsely chopped nuts

1 egg plus 1 tablespoon water (optional), for egg wash

Lemon Chess Pie

MAKES ONE 9-INCH PIE

You know a pie recipe is old when several stories are told about its history. Some say the term chess pie *goes back to an eighteenth-century English cheese pie. Another links the origins of the name to the Southern pie chest, or pie safe, a piece of furniture that holds kitchen confections. Another anecdote tells of a man who stopped to eat at a diner in Alabama. He loved the pie he was served, and when he asked what its name was, the waitress replied, "jes pie." Whatever the truth may be, as food writer Stephanie Anderson Witmer says, "So many Southern pies, like the chess pies, are elegant in their simplicity. They use staple ingredients, but are divine."*

½ recipe Plain Pie Pastry (page 17)
   or Vinegar Pie Crust (page 19)

¼ cup unsalted butter

1½ cups sugar

3 eggs

1 tablespoon cornmeal

Juice of 1½ lemons

Preheat the oven to 350°F. Line a 9-inch pie plate with the rolled-out crust. For a crispier crust, consider parbaking.

Melt butter in a saucepan over medium heat, then remove from the heat and stir in the sugar. Beat in the eggs, then stir in the cornmeal, and then the lemon juice. Pour the filling into the crust.

Bake for 35 to 45 minutes, until the filling is a deep golden brown. Cool on a wire rack for 1 hour before slicing.

Old-Fashioned Monterey Maple Syrup Pie

MAKES ONE 9-INCH PIE

Maple syrup holds a special place in the hearts of Southerners. In the village of Monterey, Virginia—known as "Little Switzerland"—the annual Maple Syrup Festival draws thousands of visitors. When gathering ingredients for this pie, it's important to note that many maple-flavored syrups are just corn syrup with maple flavoring (a shocking revelation for me!). Read the label to make certain you're getting 100 percent pure maple syrup. Grade B maple syrup is great for cooking; it has a deeper flavor and color than the Grade A amber syrup, although Grade A will work, too. Of course, maple syrup from Monterey will add a wonderful authentic note to this pie for people with a serious sweet tooth.

½ recipe Plain Pie Pastry (page 17) or Vinegar Pie Crust (page 19)

2 eggs, beaten

1 cup maple syrup

2 tablespoons unsalted butter, melted

1 cup brown sugar

½ cup walnuts

3 tablespoons all-purpose flour

Preheat the oven to 375°F. Line a 9-inch pie plate with the rolled-out crust. For a crispier crust, consider parbaking.

Combine the eggs, maple syrup, butter, brown sugar, walnuts, and flour and stir until thoroughly combined. Spread the filling evenly in the crust.

Bake for 45 to 50 minutes, until the filling forms a crust but the pie is still gooey underneath. Cool on a wire rack for 1 hour before slicing. Serve at room temperature or chilled.

INDEX